The
PRIME MOVER
of Progress

The
PRIME MOVER
of Progress

The Entrepreneur in
Capitalism and Socialism

Papers on 'The Rôle of the Entrepreneur'

ISRAEL KIRZNER

LESLIE HANNAH   ●   NEIL McKENDRICK

NIGEL VINSON   ●   KEITH WICKENDEN

SIR ARTHUR KNIGHT   ●   SIR FRANK McFADZEAN

P. D. HENDERSON   ●   D. G. MacRAE

IVOR PEARCE

Published by
The Institute of Economic Affairs
1980

First published in March 1980 by
THE INSTITUTE OF ECONOMIC AFFAIRS
© The Institute of Economic Affairs 1980

All rights reserved

ISSN 0305-814X
ISBN 0-255 36129-7

Printed in England by
Goron-Pro-Print Co. Ltd., Lancing, Sussex
Set in Monotype Times Roman 11 on 12 point

Contents

Preface

The *IEA Readings* have been devised to refine the market in economic thinking by presenting varying approaches to a single theme. They are intended primarily for teachers and students of economics but are edited to help non-economists who want to know how economics can explain their activities.

Readings 23 is based on a Seminar in October 1979 which was organised to examine the rôle of the entrepreneur in the British economy. It arose from a conviction that the long discussion of economic growth in Britain (or rather the lack of it in recent years) has largely ignored the source of the innovation that underlies it.

The opening lecture, by Professor Israel Kirzner of the USA, outlined a pure theory of entrepreneurship. ('Theory' does not denote a realm of thought remote from the real world; it is rather a reinforcement of insight by observation designed to explain the real world. The emphasis is on 'explain': a theory of entrepreneurship attempts to explain how men are moved to new activity that would be an improvement on the old.) Professor Kirzner's theory is that the source of entrepreneurship is alertness to opportunity, and the imagination and vision to exploit or capitalise on it. These qualities —their strength or weakness—explain why some societies have high rates of growth and others low rates; why some are rich and others poor. And the important implication for public policy is that 'alertness' may be nurtured or suppressed by the institutions created by society through its political government. Alertness can lead men with initiative, drive, the capacity—perhaps the impulse—to take risks with their money, their repute and their livelihood in wrestling with competitors, bargaining with suppliers, and anticipating the wants of consumers. The theory should thus explain why systems that create the widest opportunities for entrepreneurship—commonly known as 'capitalism'—are everywhere in the world richer than societies that suppress it—collectively described as varying forms of state economy, from social democracy to communism.

Professor Kirzner discusses the personal qualities that make for entrepreneurial alertness: restive temperament, a thirst for adventure, ambition and imagination. All such qualities may be nurtured or suppressed. They are presumably similar in Germany on both sides of the Iron Curtain, in Korea North and South of the 38th parallel, on both sides of the China Sea separating the Chinese mainland from the island of Taiwan. But the results are very different according to the institutions created by government. In some environments the innate urge of mankind to discover new techniques and new ideas is given freest rein in competitive markets. In others men of the same race, culture and instincts are not allowed to express these qualities. It is thus fascinating to speculate on what Russia would now be like if the economic liberalism of the decade before Lenin had continued to develop entrepreneurial alertness instead of being succeeded by state economy.

A central element of entrepreneurship analysed by Professor Kirzner must be emphasised: 'Human beings tend to notice that which it is in their interest to notice'. This is a plain, unremarkable statement of a fundamental facet of human nature. And it is true in every society. It may be deplored where it is thought to degenerate into selfishness or be applauded where it is seen as a powerful inducement to initiative. Nor is it proper to interpret 'interest' as 'self-interest', since 'interest' may include not only a man's concern with himself but also with his family, other people in his circle, and with doing good to people he would like to help.

The interesting question provoked by the succeeding discussion was: Where does the entrepreneurial function reside? Where is the entrepreneur in British Steel or British Leyland? Where is he in Russia or China? He is there somewhere, but he is not easy to identify. It is not clear who takes initiatives at whose risk: who gains, who suffers. Not least there is a clear dividing line between the systems in which entrepreneurs risk their own and those in which entrepreneurs risk other people's money. And where the instinct to notice opportunities in, say, new methods of rotating crops or welding metals or making hospital cots safe, is suppressed because it is centralised in a handful of planners, where else does the individual instinct to innovate express itself?

Professor Kirzner comes closest to current British economic policy in discussing the entrepreneurial rôle in the 'regulated market economy', roughly what is called the mixed economy of price and wage controls, incomes policy, regional aid, government-sponsored investment, subsidies to industries to maintain jobs, manipulation of nationalised industry pricing to stabilise the 'cost of living', government standards and requirements of all kinds. What remains for the supporters of such a system to demonstrate is that entrepreneurship can be exercised more effectively by politicians or bureaucrats risking public money than by individuals risking their own. It is never clear why Mr Anthony Wedgwood Benn thinks government is more capable of showing 'alertness' to opportunity than are the men on the spot with a prospect of personal gain.

The two historians, Dr Leslie Hannah of the London School of Economics, and Mr Neil McKendrick of Cambridge University, delivered fascinating reflections on entrepreneurs in British history, with observations on names that became famous 50 or 100 years ago and often remain important today. Contemporary 19th/20th century opinion as reflected in the writings of novelists often presented a caricature of entrepreneurship that remained unchallenged until the last two or three decades. (The issues here were discussed by economists and historians in *The Long Debate on Poverty*, IEA, second edition, 1974.) Entrepreneurs as individuals and industry in general have been condemned not only by intellectuals on the Left but also by romantics on the Right. (The attitude continues today in the reaction to the newest kind of entrepreneur in sport, whose activities are analysed by Professor Peter Sloane in Hobart Paper 85.) The astringent note of condemnation of the entrepreneur in British social observation and literary criticism is a strong element in the revulsion of many able young men against work in industry, and has contributed to the flagging economic performance of the British economy.

The historians were followed by three real-life entrepreneurs with 'cameos' of their experience. Mr Nigel Vinson gave an intriguing account of 'alertness'—his discovery of an unperceived opportunity leading to the creation of a new firm and a new product in plastics. At the age of 21 he 'noticed we often received inquiries we could not fulfil'; by the age of 35 he had created a substantial and prosperous firm and served many consumers in the process. His reflections on the ingredients of success and on the obstruction to entrepreneurs created by government are the stuff of industrial achievement and a warning on public policy.

Mr Keith Wickenden spoke of entrepreneurship in transport. His 'alertness' was in detecting a gap in the market for the passenger who wants to go to Europe without a car (estimated at 7 million a year). His solution was to compete with British Rail's London to Paris train service by airship (rather than helicopter) from city to city; and again his reflections on the task of raising money for a new opportunity also make intriguing reading. On the personal qualities reviewed by Professor Kirzner, Mr Wickenden said entrepreneurs had to be 'slightly nutty', to have the ability to turn bad luck into success (his account of the voucher solution to exchange control is heartening), and to be intuitive. Mr Wickenden is also self-confident enough to recount a failure—a rare revelation, as researchers know from experience.[1]

The third cameo by Sir Arthur Knight is of especial interest since he was on the point of retiring from Courtaulds and later went to the Chairmanship of the National Enterprise Board. His story was of guiding a large firm through economic shoals and emerging with new strength. Of especial interest are his observations on the five policy requirements for a widespread entrepreneurial spirit.

The fourth entrepreneur on the platform, Sir Frank McFadzean, was invited to discuss entrepreneurship in private and state industry as exemplified by Shell and British Airways. His verdict, in effect, was that in state industry entrepreneurial calculation is 'crowded off' by the vote motive. Accountability to the final consumer was therefore through a handful of politicians and bureaucrats. The purpose of nationalised industry was ill-defined: together with increased politicisation came amateurisation. Efforts to introduce marginal cost pricing had not succeeded in replacing political rhetoric. Entrepreneurship varied inversely with the degree of government intervention. Sir Frank is now Chairman of Rolls-Royce.

The final sessions on the sociology of entrepreneurship led by Professor Donald MacRae and on the public policy required to enable entrepreneurship to yield its results opened by Professor Ivor Pearce both stimulated closely-argued discussions.

The Institute is indebted to the economists, historians, sociologists and entrepreneurs both on the platform and in the audience for making the discussion and this *Readings* a stimulating assembly of authoritative review and judgement and therefore of value to teachers and students of economics in general and to industry in particular.

February 1980   ARTHUR SELDON

---

[1] Ralph Harris and Arthur Seldon, *Advertising in Action* and *Advertising and the Public*, IEA, 1962.

OPENING REMARKS

by the Chairman

ARTHUR SELDON
Institute of Economic Affairs

I welcome you to this, the 10th IEA event of its kind in the last seven years. Until the last one, we called them 'seminars', but that word rather suggested that we on the platform 'talk down' to you out there. Since this audience was chosen for its especially high quality and its blend of scholarship and experience, we have called it a Colloquium, to indicate that the platform will talk with the audience as equals.

Our subject is the rôle of the entrepreneur—what it is, what it has been, what it should be, and what it could be in raising output, living standards and in the advance of mankind generally. Never before, until recently, in the history of capitalism have so many capitalists been misused or ill-used, in Shakespeare's sense, by so many governments, of both parties, under the influence of a common error about the working of a competitive market order. Our capitalists have been alternately abused and bullied, cajoled and damned, elevated and ground down, harried and inflated, pampered and villified.

During the day we shall no doubt hear praise and blame. We all know the case of George Hudson who built, or financed, railways in the 1840s, but who also sailed near the wind. It is highly conjectural whether he did more harm than good. But I hope we shall concentrate on the analysis of why entrepreneurs do what they do, and if they do not do what we all think they ought to do, whether the fault lies at their door or at the door of politicians who should have supplied the competitive, legal framework required to enable and induce them to do their job: meeting changing demand at home and overseas.

We now turn to our keynote lecture. I regard Professor Kirzner as the most searching thinker on the rôle of the entrepreneur in economic society and a worthy successor in the long line of Austrian economists which began, roughly, with Carl Menger and came to us *via* Ludwig Mises and the man who is now the most considerable economic philosopher of our time, Friedrich Hayek.

1. The Primacy of Entrepreneurial Discovery

ISRAEL M. KIRZNER
New York University

The Author

ISRAEL M. KIRZNER: Professor of Economics, New York University, since 1968. Educated at the Universities of Cape Town, 1947-48; London, 1950-51; New York University (Ph.D., 1957). Since 1957 in the Economics Department of New York University: Assistant Professor 1957-61; Associate Professor 1961-68. Author of *The Economic Point of View* (1960); *Market Theory and the Price System* (1963); *An Essay on Capital* (1966); *Competition and Entrepreneurship* (1973); *Perception, Opportunity, and Profit* (1979).

I. INTRODUCTION

An economically successful society is one whose members pursue the 'right' set of co-ordinated actions. The 'ideal' economic organisation for a society consists, therefore, of the pattern of institutions and incentives that will promote the pursuit of the 'correct' set of actions by its members. Economic theory has, in general terms, been able to enunciate the conditions to be fulfilled if a set of actions is to be 'correct'. These optimality conditions are, not surprisingly, governed basically by the available resources and technological possibilities, on the one hand, and, on the other, by the pattern of consumers' tastes. The 'economic problem' faced by society is then often viewed as being somehow to ensure that the various economic agents in society indeed undertake those actions that will, altogether, satisfy the conditions for optimality. While this formulation is in some respects not quite satisfactory, it will serve reasonably well in introducing our discussion of the role of entrepreneurial discovery.

II. PATTERNS OF ECONOMIC ORGANISATION

In theory there exists a variety of possible patterns of economic organisation for society, ranging from completely centralised decision-making at one extreme, through an array of 'mixed' systems, to pure *laissez-faire*. Several related observations may be made.

First, *all* these possible systems of economic organisation involve making *decisions*—with greater or lesser degree of decentralisation.

Second, these decisions will necessarily involve an *entrepreneurial element*—regardless of the degree of decentralisation sought.

Third, one dimension along which the effectiveness of each of the alternative patterns of societal economic organisation will need to be assessed, will therefore be that of measuring the *success with which entrepreneurial activity can be evoked in that pattern of organisation*.

These observations call for some elaboration.

(i) The Entrepreneurial Element in Decisions

We have asserted that decisions necessarily involve an entrepreneurial element. What do we mean by the 'entrepreneurial element' in decision?

The *non*-entrepreneurial element in decisions is easy to pin down. In most textbooks of micro-economics, this non-entrepreneurial element is often made to appear the *only* element in decision-making. The non-entrepreneurial element in decision-making consists of the task of calculation. A decision-maker is, in this context, seen as seeking to achieve an array of goals (or to 'maximise' some goal or utility function) with the scarce resources available. In seeking to arrive at the optimal decision, the decision-maker must therefore calculate the solution to what, in the jargon of economics, is called a 'constrained maximisation problem'.*[1] Correct decision-making, in this non-entrepreneurial sense, means correct calculation; faulty decision-making is equivalent to mistakes in arithmetic.

This non-entrepreneurial aspect does not have to assume initial omniscience; it is entirely possible for the incompletely informed decision-maker to calculate (i.e. to decide) how much knowledge to acquire.[2] But this non-entrepreneurial aspect does presume, at least, that the decision-maker has a clear perception of the scope of his ignorance, and of how this ignorance can be reduced; in a sense he knows precisely what it is that he does not know. And it is here that we can recognise the scope for the other element in decision-making, the entrepreneurial element.

For the truth is that the calculative aspect is far from being the most obvious and most important element in decisions. When a wrong decision has been made, the error is unlikely to have been a mistake in calculation. It is far more likely to have resulted from an erroneous assessment of the situation—in being over-optimistic about the availability of means, or about the outcomes to be expected of given actions; in pessimistically under-estimating the means at one's

---

* I.e. the problem of achieving maximum desirable results without overstepping the constraints imposed by the limited resources available.

[1] This emphasis on maximisation is to be traced to the influence of Lord Robbins, *The Nature and Significance of Economic Science,* Macmillan, London, 1932.

[2] The literature on the economics of search proceeds on this basis. The classic article is G. J. Stigler, 'The Economics of Information', *Journal of Political Economy,* June 1961, pp. 213-25.

disposal, or the results to be expected from specific courses of action. Making the 'right' decision, therefore, calls for far more than the correct mathematical calculation; it calls for a shrewd and wise assessment of the realities (both present and future) within the context of which the decision must be taken. It is with this aspect of decision that we will be dealing in analysing the entrepreneurial element in subsequent discussion.

No matter how centralised or decentralised a decision-making system may be, its decision-makers will regret their decisions if the entrepreneurship embodied in these decisions is of poor quality. Whatever the institutional context, a correct decision calls for reading the situation correctly; it calls for recognising the true possibilities and for refusing to be deluded into seeing possibilities where none exist; it requires that true possibilities should not be overlooked, but that true limitations not be overlooked either. It is therefore our contention that alternative systems of economic organisations have to be appraised, in part, with an eye to the respective success with which they can evoke entrepreneurship of high quality.

(ii) Entrepreneurship in Received Economic Theory

It is by now fairly well recognised that standard economic theory has developed along lines that virtually exclude the entrepreneurial rôle. This has largely been a result of the tendencies, long dominant in neo-classical economics, to exclude all elements of unexpected change, to focus attention almost exclusively on equilibrium states of affairs, and to treat individual decisions as immune from the hazards of error.[3]

As Frank Knight of Chicago explained many years ago, in a world from which the troublesome demon of unexpected change has been exorcised, it is not difficult to imagine away any need for entrepreneurship.[4] In such a world we can reasonably expect decision-makers, given sufficient time, to have come somehow to perceive the world correctly. To decide, in such a world, involves nothing more than to perform those calculations which we have described as constituting the non-entrepreneurial element in decision-making.

---

[3] An elaboration of this theme is in the author's *Competition and Entrepreneurship,* University of Chicago Press, Chicago and London, 1973, Chapters 1-3.

[4] F. H. Knight, *Risk, Uncertainty and Profit,* Houghton Mifflin, Boston, 1921.

In a world of unchanging certainty, where the future unfolding of events is anticipated with assurance and accuracy, selecting the optimal course of action is not a task which challenges the entrepreneurial qualities of vision, daring, and determination. Indeed, it is difficult to imagine how such a world could ever fail to be in anything but a state of optimality. To be sure, such a world must be envisaged as bounded by resource scarcities. But it is difficult to imagine how anyone in such a world—given these resource limitations, and given the accepted structure of ownership—can ascribe any perceived short-comings to faulty decision-making. Such an imaginary world is not paradise, but it can hardly fail to be the closest to paradise imaginable within the given limitations of supply and the given institutional framework.

When this theoretical framework is uncritically adopted, it becomes easy to fall into the error of tackling economic problems with non-entrepreneurial analytical tools. It becomes natural to assume that the correct decisions are being made, from the viewpoint of the relevant decision-makers; that the problems encountered are to be attributed to inadequate resources or to a faulty institutional structure. What is overlooked, in such treatments, is the possibility that a great deal of want and misery are the result of nothing less mundane than *sheer error* on the part of decision-makers, that is, of decisions made that, from the decision-maker's *own* point of view, are sub-optimal. That such errors may and do occur requires us to recognise scope for entrepreneurial error, for decisions made with faulty assessments of the facts of the world, future as well as present, upon which the decision is to impinge.

Certainly, in a perspective which simply assumes that decision-makers, under all circumstances, regardless of institutional environment, inevitably and unerringly find their way to the correct decisions—there is little point in inquiring into the circumstances that are most conducive to alert, entrepreneurially-successful decision-making. It is a fundamental insight upon which, I believe, the proceedings of today's Colloquium are being conducted, that simply to assume correct decision-making is to beg far too large a fraction of the essential question confronting us. We begin, in other words, with a healthy awareness that the world is very far from being the best of all possible worlds—even from being the best of those worlds possible with available resources, and within existing institutional environments.

It is from this beginning that we are led to appreciate the primordial importance of our question: What institutional circumstances or arrangements, which system of economic and political institutions, can be expected most successfully to evoke those qualities of entrepreneurial alertness upon which the quest for optimality in decision-making necessarily depends?

(iii) ENTREPRENEURSHIP AS A SCARCE RESOURCE

It might perhaps be argued that, important as the quality of entrepreneurship undoubtedly is, it does not involve any really new considerations beyond those usually taken into account in studying the conditions for optimality. All that has been established in the preceding pages, it may be held, is merely that we must bear in mind the need for a special resource, entrepreneurship, which has often been incorrectly taken for granted. Instead of viewing entrepreneurship as exercised flawlessly, tirelessly, and universally, we must begin to recognise that it is a scarce, valuable resource of which our economic models had better begin to take careful account. But all this, it may perhaps be maintained, does not justify our demand that we transcend the standard maximising model of decision-making. All that has to be done, it may be contended, is to incorporate into our list of required resources the flow of required entrepreneurial services, and to ensure that available stocks of such service flows be used optimally. Social optimality, it may be contended, will now be judged within a broader framework in which there is recognition of both the demand for, and availability of, the service of entrepreneurial vision.

More particularly, in respect of the question we have described as primordial, it may be objected that it is fundamentally inappropriate to inquire into the comparative effectiveness of alternative institutional frameworks, for the evocation of entrepreneurship. It will be objected that, since entrepreneurship is a resource no different, for pure theory, from other resources, any comparison among alternative social economic systems must begin with the assumption of some *given,* initial stock of that resource. It will not do to begin a comparison between different economic systems by suggesting that the very pattern of institutional arrangement may have important implications for the initial size of a particular stock of resource. Different economic systems may certainly differ in the efficiency with which they deploy and allocate given resource supplies; but, it may be argued, if we postulate some given supply of a particular resource in one economic system, there can be no objection in principle to supposing any other system to begin with exactly the same supply of that resource.

Our response to this line of argument (and thus our defence of the validity of the central question to be addressed here) rests on the insight that entrepreneurship cannot usefully be treated simply as a resource, similar in principle to the other resources available to an economic system.

III. THE PRIMACY OF ENTREPRENEURSHIP

What is important is to insist that entrepreneurial alertness differs in fundamental respects from the resources ordinarily discussed in decision-making. These differences will justify our contention that there may be important differences between different economic systems in respect of their success in harnessing entrepreneurial alertness for making error-free decisions.

A cardinal quality of a potential resource, in the economists' analysis of decisions, is that the decision-maker can deploy it, if he so chooses, in specific processes geared toward the achievement of specified goals. What the decision-maker has to decide is whether to deploy a particular resource, how and in what quantity to deploy it. He must decide whether to use it at all, whether to use it for one purpose or for another. The quality of entrepreneurial alertness cannot be discussed in these terms.

Entrepreneurial alertness is not a conventional economic resource

If an entrepreneur's discovery of a lucrative arbitrage opportunity galvanizes him into immediate action to capture the perceived gain, it will not do to describe the situation as one in which the entrepreneur has 'decided' to use his alertness in order to capture this gain. He has not 'deployed' his hunch for a specific purpose; *rather, his hunch has propelled him to make his entrepreneurial purchase and sale.* The entrepreneur never sees his hunches as potential inputs about which he must decide whether or not they are to be used. To decide *not* to use a hunch means—if it means anything at all—that a businessman realises that he has no hunch (or that his hunch is that it will be best to be inactive for the time being). If one has become sufficiently alerted to the existence of an opportunity—i.e., if one has become sufficiently convinced regarding the facts of a situation—it becomes virtually impossible to imagine *not* taking advantage of the opportunity so discovered.

Entrepreneurship is thus not something to be deliberately introduced into a potential production process; it is, instead, something primordial to the very idea of a potential production process awaiting possible implementation. Entrepreneurial alertness is not an ingredient *to be deployed* in decision-making; it is rather something in which *the decision itself is embedded* and without which it would be unthinkable.

It is true that *knowledge* (e.g., in the sense of technical expertise) may be deployed. A person may certainly decide that it does not pay to use his knowledge in a specific manner. Or he may decide that it does pay to use it. Here knowledge is a resource at the disposal of the entrepreneur. He is conscious of his knowledge as something to be used or not. But this refers only to knowledge of how to achieve specific goals, not knowledge of whether or not it is worthwhile to attempt to achieve a goal altogether. A distinguishing feature of entrepreneurial insight consists precisely in the absence of self-awareness by its possessor that he does possess it. A would-be entrepreneur may agonise over whether or not to embark on a particular venture. His trauma arises not from deciding whether or not to use his entrepreneurial vision; it stems from his unsureness of what he 'sees'.

Entrepreneurial opportunity may be blocked by lack of a resource but not of insight

Again, it is integral to a necessary resource (in the usual sense) that a decision-maker may feel its lack. A decision-maker may say: 'I have all the ingredients necessary to produce ice-cream, except sugar'. The opportunity to achieve a particular goal is blocked only by lack of some necessary resource. But it is absurd to imagine a decision-maker saying (on a commercial venture about the profitability of which he is profoundly sceptical) that he sees a profitable opportunity the exploitation of which is blocked only by lack of entrepreneurial insight. It would be absurd because this entrepreneur is (correctly or otherwise) convinced that he does *not* see any profitable opportunity in this venture at all.

To repeat what was stated earlier, all this does not apply to *technical* knowledge which an entrepreneur may know exists and which he knows he lacks. It is certainly possible for a decision-maker to say: 'I have all the ingredients for ice-cream, but I lack the relevant recipe'. He may know that a recipe exists, and that it is a good one, without knowing what it is. But for a man to refrain from a particular productive venture because he is not convinced that it is sound—even if it turns out that he was wrong—is not to refrain from it because he has been unable to lay hands on the appropriate vision; it is to refrain because he is convinced (rightly or wrongly) that, with respect to this venture, the *best entrepreneurial alertness finds nothing to be seen.*

Entrepreneurial alertness is not a potential stock available to society

It is because of this inherent *primacy* of entrepreneurial alertness and vision (as contrasted with deployable resources)[5] that we cannot avoid the question to be addressed in this paper—the varying degrees of success with which alternative economic systems can inspire entrepreneurial alertness. We do not view the *potential* stock of entrepreneurial alertness in a society as some quantity 'available to be used by society'. (Were this the case one could proceed to inquire how different systems variously succeed in most effectively using this uniformly *given* stock.) Instead we recognise the quality of entrepreneurial alertness as something which *somehow emerges into view at the precise moment when decisions have to be made.* As we shall see (VII), this opens up the important possibility that the institutional framework within which decisions are made may itself vitally affect the alertness out of which those decisions emerge.

---

[5] A fuller discussion of this insight is in the author's *Perception, Opportunity, and Profit,* University of Chicago Press, Chicago and London, 1979, Chapters 9, 10.

IV. THE COST OF ENTREPRENEURSHIP

This line of argument points to a further related insight: *entrepreneurship is costless*. In using any quantity of a scarce resource (in the usual sense of that term) the decision-maker is always viewed as choosing between alternative goals to which the scarce resource might be applied. The goal foregone is the cost of using the resource for its present purpose. In the case of entrepreneurial alertness, however, a decision-maker never considers whether to apply some given potential alertness to the discovery of opportunity A or opportunity B. As already argued, the opportunities (or any one of them) are either perceived or they are not perceived; alertness is not something about which a decision can be made *not* to deploy it. (In this we distinguish sharply between pure alertness, on the one hand, and 'deployable' scarce inputs that may be useful in decision-making, e.g., time, technical knowledge, managerial expertise, on the other.) To recognise that opportunity A exists need not preclude simultaneously recognising that opportunity B exists.

Conversely, to fail to recognise that opportunity A exists cannot be explained in terms of the high cost of so recognising it; if opportunity A has not been recognised, the failure represents some shortcoming in entrepreneurial alertness, not the outcome of a decision to deploy it for the discovery of other opportunities.

Faulty entrepreneurship means alertness remains untapped

That in the real world we encounter innumerable instances of faulty and inadequate entrepreneurship must be interpreted, therefore, not as evidence of the absolute scarcity of entrepreneurial alertness (with the existing stock of it having been applied elsewhere), but as evidence that the alertness costlessly available has somehow remained latent and untapped. The central question then looms even more significantly than ever: What institutional frameworks are best suited to tap the reservoir of entrepreneurial alertness which is certainly present—in potentially inexhaustible supply—among the members of society?

V. THE QUALITIES OF ENTREPRENEURSHIP— THE UNCHARTED FRONTIER

Although, as Ludwig von Mises pointed out long ago,[6] *all* individual action is entrepreneurial, and although we have described entrepreneurial alertness as in principle inexhaustible, we have also been careful to notice that potential alertness may be (and so often is) untapped and inert. We know, certainly, that individuals display vastly different degrees of entrepreneurial alertness. Some are quick to spot as yet unnoticed opportunities, others notice only the opportunities revealed by the discoveries of others. In some societies, in some climates, among some groups, it appears that entrepreneurial alertness is keener than in others. Studies of economic development have come to recognise that the qualities called for in successful entrepreneurship are not uniformly distributed, and certainly do not appear to be in infinite supply.

It would certainly be desirable to be able to identify with precision those human qualities, personal and psychological, which are to be credited with successful entrepreneurial alertness, drive and initiative. It would be most valuable to be able to study the short-run and long-run impact upon the development of these 'entrepreneurial' qualities, of alternative social, economic and institutional frameworks. It would be important to know, for example, if a comfortable sense of security discourages the noticing of new opportunities. If 'independence' or 'economic freedom' encourages entrepreneurial drive and initiative, this would be significant information. Likewise, does 'competition' encourage alertness to new opportunities?

Research on psychological aspects desirable

Up to the present, little systematic work appears to have been done on these questions. Observations made are likely to be based on 'common sense' or on anecdotal foundations. It is certainly necessary to go beyond this elementary stage. Indeed, an important frontier of knowledge, largely unexplored, appears to consist of those aspects of psychology such as temperament, thirst for adventure, ambition and imagination that are likely to throw light on the development of the qualities of entrepreneurship, and on the ways in which alternative institutional arrangements may affect such development.

---

[6] In *Human Action,* Yale University Press, New Haven, 1949, p. 253.

It is to be expected and very much to be desired that research should proceed on this frontier during the years ahead.

Applied entrepreneurial theorists should look to this research with considerable interest; it is to be hoped that their own needs and interests will help to define the directions along which this research proceeds and to formulate the questions it seeks to answer.

My tentative observations here will suggest that a number of important general statements can be made even before we enjoy the systematic knowledge anticipated to emerge from research into the psychology of entrepreneurship.

VI. THE INCENTIVE FOR ENTREPRENEURIAL DISCOVERY

Were entrepreneurship a scarce resource in the usual sense, economists would have no difficulty in spelling out, at least in general terms, the kinds of incentives capable of coaxing out the desired quantity of entrepreneurial discovery. Potential entrepreneurs would have to be offered rewards that more than offset the costs of exercising entrepreneurship. This, after all, is how economists understand the role of incentives; this is how the price system is perceived to offer, *via* the resource market, the incentives required to stimulate resource supply and to allocate it among alternative uses. But the special aspects of entrepreneurship render this kind of incentive system inappropriate to entrepreneurial alertness and discovery.

Since entrepreneurship is costless (no incentive at all is needed, in principle, to activate entrepreneurial vision), and since on the other hand entrepreneurial vision is not uniformly and continuously 'switched on' to take advantage of all opportunities, we are very much concerned to identify what it is that *does* 'switch on' entrepreneurial vision and discovery.

With scarce resources in the usual sense, it is meaningful to talk of the kind of incentive needed to be 'offered' to owners to stimulate supply. We can imagine, that is, that some entrepreneur already has a fairly clear picture of the results to be obtained from deploying the relevant resource in some particular line of production. We can then talk of whether or not it is worthwhile for him to offer the resource price required to overcome the cost of supplying the resource. The point is that the notion of a needed incentive, in this usual sense, presupposes the clear perception, even before the deployment of the service, of its usefulness in production.

As has already been emphasised (p. 15), such a perception is ruled out by definition in the case of entrepreneurial alertness. No-one 'hires' or 'offers incentives' to the entrepreneur. To hire an 'entrepreneur' *is to be an entrepreneur*—simply shifting the problem back to the incentives that might galvanize *this* latter entrepreneur into action. It cannot be sufficiently emphasised that

(a) until an opportunity *has* been discovered, no one knows how much to offer as an incentive for its discovery;

(b) once the opportunity has been discovered, it is no longer relevant to inquire into the springs of entrepreneurship—since it will already have been exercised.

The promise of pure gain is entrepreneurial incentive

There seems one statement which, however, can be made about the incentives required to excite entrepreneurial alertness. It is a statement which sees such incentives as having little in common with the character of and rôle for incentives in the usual sense. It can be stated with considerable confidence *that human beings tend to notice that which it is in their interest to notice.* Human beings notice 'opportunities' rather than 'situations'. They notice, that is, concatenations of events, realised or prospective, which offer *pure gain*. It is not the abstract *concatenation* of these events which evokes notice; it is the circumstance that these events offer the promise of pure *gain*—broadly understood to include fame, power, prestige, even the opportunity to serve a cause or to help other individuals.

Two individuals walk through the same city block teeming with hundreds of people in a variety of garbs, with shops of different kinds, advertising signs for many goods, buildings of different architectural styles. Each of these individuals will notice a different set of items out of these countless impressions impinging on his senses. What is noticed by the one is not what is noticed by the other. The difference will not merely be one of chance. It is a difference that can be ascribed, in part, to the *interests* of the two individuals. Each tends to notice that which is of interest *to him*.

A difference between the price of apples traded in one part of the market and the price of apples traded in another part may pass unnoticed. It is less likely to pass unnoticed if it constitutes a phenomenon of interest to its potential discoverer. A concatenation of possible events (in this case the possible purchase of apples at a lower price, to be followed by their sale at a higher price) may not be noticed at all unless the potential discoverer stands to gain from the price differential. *In order to 'switch on' the alertness of a potential discoverer to socially significant opportunities, they must offer gain to the potential discoverer himself.*

This kind of incentive—the incentive that somehow converts a socially desirable opportunity into a personally gainful one—is not needed to ensure pursuit of that opportunity *after* its discovery. Once the socially desirable opportunity has been perceived, individuals may be persuaded (or threatened) to act on that opportunity simply by suitable choice of reward (or punishment). The kind of incentive here under discussion is that required to reveal opportunities that have *until now been perceived by no-one at all.*

VII. PERFORMANCE OF ALTERNATIVE ECONOMIC SYSTEMS UNDER ENTREPRENEURIAL INCENTIVE

How do alternative social-economic systems appear likely to perform in terms of this kind of incentive? We will consider (a) a free market economy, (b) a centralised (socialist) economic system, (c) a regulated market economy. Our concern is solely with the comparative scope they hold for entrepreneurial incentives.

(a) ENTREPRENEURSHIP IN THE FREE MARKET

The free market is characterised most distinctively, for our purpose, *by freedom of entrepreneurial entry.* Given some accepted system of property rights, individual participants are free to enter into mutually beneficial trades with each other. Production decisions involve judgements about buying inputs on factor markets in order to sell output in product markets. Market prices therefore guide the decisions which determine the allocation of society's resources among alternative lines of output. Were the market to have attained full equilibrium, it may, under specific assumptions, be described as having attained an optimal allocation of resources.[7] But (especially in view of ambi-

---

[7] A complete discussion of this central theorem of welfare economics is in W. J. Baumol, *Economic Theory and Operations Analysis,* Prentice Hall, Englewood Cliffs, New Jersey, 4th Edition, 1977, Chapter 21.

guities surrounding the interpretation of 'social optimum', and of the possibility that not all the specific assumptions will be fulfilled in practice) this is *not* the interesting proposition—even were it reasonable to view the free market economy as in continuous equilibrium.

What is important about the market economy is that unexploited opportunities for re-allocating resources from one (low-market-valued) use to another of higher value offer the opportunity for pure entrepreneurial gain. A misallocation of resources occurs because, so far, market participants have not noticed the price discrepancy involved. This price discrepancy presents itself as an opportunity to be exploited by its discoverer. *The most impressive aspect of the market system is the tendency for such opportunities to be discovered.*

The discovery process of the market

It is in a sense similar to this that Hayek has referred to the competitive market process as a 'discovery procedure'.[8] The essence is not that market prices offer spontaneously developed 'signals' able fault-lessly to co-ordinate millions of independently-made decisions. (This would occur only in equilibrium; in disequilibrium the prices which prevail would *not* so perfectly co-ordinate decisions.) It is rather that the disequilibrium situation—in which prices do not offer the correct signals—is one which offers entrepreneurs the required incentives for the discrepancies to be noticed and corrected. In the course of this entrepreneurial process, new products may be introduced, new qualities of existing products may be developed, new methods of production may be ventured, new forms of industrial organisation, financing, marketing or tackling risk may be developed. All the ceaseless churning and agitation of the market is to be understood as the consequence of the never-ending discovery process of which the market consists.

(b) Entrepreneurship in the Socialised Economy

Little work has been done on the analysis of entrepreneurship in fully socialised societies. The great debate on economic calculation under socialism carried on between the two world wars, in many

---

[8] F. A. Hayek, 'Competition as a Discovery Procedure', in *New Studies in Philosophy, Politics, Economics and the History of Ideas,* University of Chicago Press, Chicago, and Routledge & Kegan Paul, London, 1978.

respects revolved precisely around this issue, but was couched in terms which unfortunately permitted the central importance of this issue to be overlooked. The attempts by Oskar Lange (of Poland) and others to show how a socialist system could be set up that would permit decentralised decisions by managers of socialist enterprises on the basis of centrally promulgated 'prices', along the same lines as the price system under the free market, unfortunately completely overlooked the entrepreneurial character of the price system.

Lange relied on the so-called 'parametric function' of prices, i.e., on that aspect of prices which permits each decision-maker to treat them as equilibrium prices to which he must passively adjust himself.[9] But in this view of the market (and hence of the possibility of a socialist 'price' system), Lange failed to recognise that the distinctive aspect of the market is the manner in which prices *change,* i.e., that market prices are in fact treated non-parametrically. It is one thing to imagine that socialist managers can be motivated to obey rules on the basis of centrally promulgated 'prices'; it is quite another to take it for granted that the *non*-parametric function of price (in which, that is, price is *not* being treated as a datum but subject to change by individual market participants), a function which depends entirely on entrepreneurial discovery of *new* opportunities for pure profit, can be simulated in a system from which the private entrepreneurial function is completely absent.

Alertness by 'price' planners and plant managers

Under a Lange-type system, alertness would be called for at a number of levels. Officials deciding on the 'price' structure must do so by what they know about the performance of the economy under earlier 'price' structures, and by what they anticipate to be the pattern of consumer demand and of resource supply in the period ahead. In promulgating a list of 'prices' it is necessary to determine, first of

---

[9] Oskar Lange, 'On the Economic Theory of Socialism', in Lange and Fred. M. Taylor, *On the Economic Theory of Socialism,* ed. Benjamin E. Lippincott, McGraw-Hill, New York, 1964, p. 70. The initial statement by Mises, demonstrating the problems in socialist economic calculation, was 'Die Wirtschaftsrechnung im sozialistischen Gemeinwesen', *Archiv für Sozialwissenschaften und Sozialpolitik* (April 1920), translated in Friedrich A. Hayek (ed.), *Collectivist Economic Planning*, Routledge and Kegan Paul, 1935. Hayek's own response to Lange is contained in his *Individualism and Economic Order,* Routledge and Kegan Paul, London, 1949.

all, the list of commodities and of resource services for which 'prices' are to be set. The construction of this list requires an enormous volume of entrepreneurial alertness on the part of these officials. After all, some products should not be produced at all; others very definitely ought to be produced, but officials may be quite ignorant of them or of their urgency. This will of course be more particularly likely to be true of new and innovative products and product qualities. But it could occur with any product whatever.

Again, the Lange system would call for alertness by socialist plant managers. They would have to identify sources of resource supply; they would have to notice technological possibilities that may not hitherto have been known, or which, given the old price structure, may not have been economic. They would have to notice the need for and possibility of any number of changes (innovative or otherwise) which changed patterns of tastes, for example, might make worthwhile. There is certainly nothing in Lange's own description of his system to suggest how this might be ensured.

Will available options be noticed? How?

The question which the entrepreneurial theorist must ask is not whether, given available known options, the relevant socialist official is operating under an incentive system that will make it personally gainful for him to select the optimal course of action for society. Our question is rather whether there is any assurance that relevant options will in practice be noticed as being available. What might motivate an official to notice an opportunity not yet adopted (but which it might be highly valuable to pursue)? It will not do to suggest that some higher official arrange matters so that, when the (lower) official does notice the opportunity, he can personally benefit by its adoption. This merely passes our question up the line: What might motivate this higher official to notice the opportunity?—and even to notice its worthwhileness *after* it has been brought to his attention?

We will, for the present, ignore the question of how a newly discovered valuable social opportunity is revealed, even after the event, as having been such. Our question will confine itself to asking how it might be ensured that such social opportunities constitute at the same time privately gainful opportunities for their potential discoverers. It is doubtful in the extreme if ideals such as benevolence or patriotism can be relied upon, in general, to enable a potential discoverer to identify his own personal interest with that of the discovery of an opportunity for a desirable re-allocation of resources for society.

We might imagine, of course, a system in which there is not merely decentralisation of decision-making, in the Lange sense, but also freedom for socialist managers to buy and sell on behalf of the state (when discrepancies among socialist 'prices' might have been discovered) and to retain for themselves some fraction of the price-differential. If such trading is restricted to those who are already socialist managers, we will have to examine the mechanism of selection of managers to see whether it indeed ensures that those with entrepreneurial skills tend to become socialist managers (since the socialist state would not be permitting others to 'prove' their entrepreneurial skills in this way). On the other hand, if entrepreneurial trading is to be open for all (raising, let us of course note, the obvious question of access to society's capital to be risked in such ventures), then clearly we have moved closer and closer toward a 'mixed' capitalist system in which private entrepreneurs might be free to seek profits within a system of state-controlled prices (a regulated system which will be briefly considered at (c), p. 23).

Individual decision-makers cannot profit under 'market' socialist schemes

We may talk of various schemes for 'market' socialism along Lange lines, in which some decisions are left to lower-ranking officials to be made on the basis of centrally-designed systems of 'prices'. No matter how extensive the degree of decentralisation thus achieved, however, a critical condition for the socialist quality of the system appears to be that neither at the level of the central design of 'prices', nor of individual-manager decisions made on the basis of these 'prices', may decisions be made primarily in order that the decision-taker can profit personally from errors discovered. Those responsible for designing the system of socialist 'prices' are clearly not participants in any entrepreneurial market; their function is to impose 'prices' upon the socialist 'market'.

To imagine that in this socialist 'market', freedom of entry for private profit-making entrepreneurial activity is to be permitted, is surely to compromise fatally the definition of a socialist economic system. But without such freedom of entrepreneurial entry market-socialism has a fatal flaw: it has not succeeded in identifying any way by which errors, whether of omission or commission, can be systematically avoided by decision-makers. It has not identified any way by which the discovery and avoidance of error redounds directly to the personal benefit of the discoverer. It has not identified how the unsuspectedly inefficient socialist venture might so reveal itself to a socialist decision-maker in advance as a threat to his own well-being; it has not identified how the currently undreamed-of venture, of critical benefit to society, might reveal itself to a socialist planner as one offering him personal gain.

Incentives to socialist managers deny essential role of entrepreneurial discovery

We do not deny the possibility of arranging incentives to socialist managers to produce more, or to produce with a smaller labour force, or lower energy consumption. Nor do we even deny the possibility of offering incentives that will reward innovation. Incentives can certainly be structured to reward inventors and innovators of new products and new production techniques. Recent extensive study of innovation in the Soviet Union has, for example, confirmed the significant vitality of the innovative process there (although the process lags more or less behind that in capitalist economies).[10] But to reward managers for meeting or exceeding target output quantities presupposes that *it is already known* that more of these outputs is urgently required by society; to reward managers for introducing a new product is to presume that *it is already known* that this particular new product—or else that *any* new product—is socially more important (taking into account the resources required for its production) than the product it replaces; to reward managers for introducing innovative methods of production is to presume that *it is already known* that the additional inputs called for by the new technique are less costly to society than those the technique avoids— or else that *any* change in production technique must be an improvement over those currently employed.

That these matters may already be known is in many instances entirely plausible. But if they *are* assumed already known, we are

---

[10] Josph S. Berliner, *The Innovation Decision in Soviet Industry,* The MIT Press, Cambridge, Mass., 1976.

simply assuming away the need for entrepreneurial discovery. The task is to ensure the discovery—by someone, somewhere, who possesses power to set things into motion—of which products (existing or new) should be produced (and in what quantities), the urgency of which the currently conventional wisdom has *failed* to recognise. The problem is to identify techniques of production the usefulness of which has up until now *not* been perceived. Not all innovation is socially desirable; not all expansion of lines of output is socially desirable. What is required is an incentive system to convince decision-makers that when they discover opportunities which others will deny to exist, they (the discoverers) will be the gainers.

Thus far, in all the discussion of varieties of socialism, of incentive systems and planning theories, we have not seen *this* problem addressed. Nor is it at all apparent how, without fundamentally compromising the essential defining criteria for socialism, it can be solved.

(c) ENTREPRENEURSHIP IN THE REGULATED MARKET ECONOMY[11]

Most societies in the modern world have allowed their economic systems to follow the pattern neither of pure socialism nor of pure capitalism. They consist of market economies that have been circumscribed by more or less extensive systems of state intervention. Convinced that the unhampered market will generate undesirable price structures, or undesirable arrays of output qualities, working conditions, or other undesirables, the state intervened, replacing the *laissez-faire* market by the regulated market. Price ceilings and price and wage floors, transfer of income, imposed safety standards, child labour laws, zoning laws, prohibited industrial integration, prohibited competition, imposed health warnings, compulsory old-age pensions, and prohibited drugs, are among the countless controls that possibly well-meaning public officials impose. What is the role of entrepreneurial discovery in the regulated market?

Genuine—but inhibited—entrepreneurial incentive

Despite the controls, regulations and interventions, there exist, in such systems, genuine markets for both resource services and con-

---

[11] Further discussion of this theme is in the author's *The Perils of Regulation: A Market-Process Approach,* Occasional Paper of the Law and Economics Center of the University of Miami School of Law, 1978.

sumer products. Although the prices which emerge in regulated markets may have been more or less drastically distorted in the regulatory process, they are (except for directly controlled prices) nonetheless market prices. To the extent that entrepreneurial entry remains free, discrepancies in these prices provide the incentives for entrepreneurs to capture pure profit, leading to a process of entrepreneurial competition acting at all times to modify the existing price structure.

Nevertheless, it is not difficult to perceive the many ways in which entrepreneurial discovery may come to be inhibited or redirected under regulatory constraints. And regulation raises new and important questions concerning the way in which the agents of the state (whether legislators or officials in other stages of regulation and its enforcement) come to notice where opportunities for supposedly beneficial regulation may exist. Let us take up these latter questions first.

Knowledge and discovery absent in price setting and resource allocation

Government regulation takes the general form of imposed price floors, price ceilings, mandated quality specifications, and similar measures. We will assume that the hope surrounding such governmental impositions is that they will confine market activities to desired channels and at desired levels. But it is by no means clear how officials will know what prices to set, or if their earlier decisions have been in error. It is not clear how officials will *discover* those opportunities for improving the allocation of resources (which, after all, we can hardly assume to be automatically known at the outset of a regulatory endeavour). The regulator's estimates of the prices consumers are prepared to pay, or of the prices resource owners are prepared to accept, are not *profit-motivated* estimates. But estimates of market demand conditions, or of market supply conditions, that are not profit-motivated cannot reflect the powerful, discovery-inspiring incentives of the entrepreneurial quest for profit.

It is, further, not clear how it can be ensured that government officials who perceive market conditions more accurately than others, will tend systematically to replace less competent regulators. It is not clear what proxy for entrepreneurial profit and loss there might be, that could inspire officials to see personal gain for themselves in successful discovery. What regulators know (or believe they know) at a given moment is presumably only partly correct. No systematic process seems available through which regulators might come to discover that which they have not known, especially since they have not known that they enjoy less than complete awareness of relevant situations. *If they do not know what they do not know, how will they know what remains to be discovered?*

Quite apart from the question of the entrepreneurship required to engage in regulation believed to be desirable, we must, in the context of the regulated market economy, also consider the impact of regulation upon the pattern and direction of entrepreneurial discovery in the market-place. There is a serious likelihood that regulatory constraints may bar the discovery of pure profit opportunities (and thus of possibilities for socially beneficial resource re-allocation).

Damaging effects of regulatory controls and price ceilings

A good deal of regulation consists in creating *barriers to entry*. Tariffs, licensing requirements, labour legislation, airline regulation, and bank regulation, for example, do not merely limit numbers in particular markets. These kinds of regulatory activity tend to bar entry to entrepreneurs who believe they have discovered profit opportunities in barred areas of the market. Such barriers may, by removing the personal gain which entrepreneurs might have reaped by their discoveries, bring it about that *some opportunities may simply not be discovered by anyone.* An entrepreneur who knows that he will not be able to enter the banking business may simply not notice opportunities in the banking field that might otherwise have seemed obvious to him; those who are already in banking, and who have failed to see these opportunities, may continue to overlook them. Protection from entrepreneurial competition does not provide any spur to entrepreneurial discovery.

Imposed price ceilings may, similarly, not merely generate disco-ordination in the markets for existing goods and services (as is of course well recognised in the theory of price controls); they may inhibit the discovery of wholly new opportunities. A price ceiling does not merely block the upper reaches of a given supply curve—further increases in supply to meet demand. It may also inhibit the discovery of as yet unsuspected sources of supply (which in the absence of the ceiling might have shifted the entire supply curve to the right—made supplies marketable at lower prices—as these sources came to be discovered), or of wholly unknown new products.

The imposition of price ceilings, which has switched off the lure of pure profits in this way, is not accompanied, as far as can be seen, by any device that might, in some alternative manner, lead a potential discoverer to associate a discovery with his own personal gain.

VIII. CONCLUSION

Our discussion has focussed attention on a neglected aspect of economic decision-making, the urgency for incentives for the 'entrepreneurial' discovery of what opportunities exist for economic action. Pursuing this point further, we have pointed to the need for critical assessment, within any economic system of organisation, of the way in which the system permits the potential discoverers to identify their own personal interest with the successful discovery of socially desirable opportunities for change. In the briefest possible framework, we have considered aspects of the socialist system, and of the regulated market economy, in contrast to the *laissez-faire* market system.

A great deal of work is waiting to be done in the economics of entrepreneurship. It has been my purpose to emphasise the enormous stake which society—under whatever economic system it may operate—holds in the successful pursuit of such research.

BIBLIOGRAPHY

Armentano, Dominic T., 'Resource Allocation Problems Under Socialism', in William P. Snavely (ed.), *Theory of Economic Systems: Capitalism, Socialism, Corporatism,* Merrill, Columbus, Ohio, 1969.

Hayek, Friedrich A. (ed.), *Collectivist Economic Planning,* Routledge and Kegan Paul, London, 1935.

——, 'Competition as a Discovery Procedure', in *New Studies in*

Philosophy, Politics, Economics and the History of Ideas, University of Chicago Press, Chicago, 1978.

——, 'Economics and Knowledge', *Economica* 4 (February 1937), pp. 33-54; reprinted in *Individualism and Economic Order.*

——, *Individualism and Economic Order,* University of Chicago Press, Chicago, 1948.

——, 'The Meaning of Competition', in *Individualism and Economic Order.*

——, 'The New Confusion About "Planning" ', *Morgan Guarantee Survey,* January 1976.

—— (ed.), 'The Nature and History of the Problem', in *Collectivist Economic Planning;* reprinted as 'Socialist Calculation I: The Nature and History of the Problem', in *Individualism and Economic Order.*

—— (ed.), 'The Present State of the Debate', in *Collectivist Economic Planning;* reprinted as 'Socialist Calculation II: The State of the Debate (1935)', in *Individualism and Economic Order.*

——, 'Socialist Calculation: The Competitive "Solution" ', *Economica* 7 (May 1940), pp. 125-149; reprinted as 'Socialist Calculation III: The Competitive "Solution" ', in *Individualism and Economic Order.*

——, 'The Use of Knowledge in Society', *American Economic Review* 35 (September 1945), pp. 519-530; reprinted in *Individualism and Economic Order.*

Hoff, Trygve J. B., *Economic Calculation in the Socialist Society,* trans. M. A. Michael, Hodge, London and Edinburgh, 1949.

Kirzner, Israel M., *Competition and Entrepreneurship,* University of Chicago Press, Chicago, 1973.

——, *Perception, Opportunity, and Profit,* University of Chicago Press, Chicago, 1979.

Lange, Oskar, 'On the Economic Theory of Socialism', in Lange, Oskar, and Taylor, Fred M., *On the Economic Theory of Socialism,* edited by Benjamin E. Lippincott, McGraw-Hill, New York, 1964.

Littlechild, Stephen C., *The Fallacy of the Mixed Economy: An 'Austrian' Critique of Economic Thinking and Policy,* Hobart Paper 80, Institute of Economic Affairs, London, 1978.

Mises, Ludwig von, 'Die Wirtschaftsrechnung im sozialistischen Gemeinwesen', *Archiv für Sozialwissenschaften und Sozialpolitik* (April 1920); reprinted in Hayek (ed.), *Collectivist Economic Planning* (1935), pp. 87-130.

——, *Human Action: A Treatise on Economics*, Yale University Press, New Haven, 1949.

Rothbard, Murray N., 'Ludwig von Mises and Economic Calculation Under Socialism', in Lawrence S. Moss (ed.), *The Economics of Ludwig von Mises,* Sheed and Ward, Kansas City, 1976.

Questions and Discussion

PROF. Z. GURZYSKI (*Professor of Economics at University of Cape Town, now at the London School of Economics*): It seems to me that the key to Professor Kirzner's extremely important address is that the entrepreneur must be able to execute his hunch. Now this depends on the institutional structure. It is possible—and this is true of the less developed countries—that the institutional structure is not favourable to entrepreneurship, and that this affects entrepreneurship itself since alertness is then diverted to those values which are important in that society, i.e. the promotion of its aristocratic structure.

This is not a matter of psychology; it is a form of amortisation à la McClelland. The basic difference seems to be between communalism and individualism, where communalism depends on the entrepreneurship of the leader and the willing following by the members who find satisfaction in the leader's approval 'on behalf of the community', whereas under individualism, the entrepreneurship is individual for individual gain. Thus a socialist system is clearly designed to be communal, whereas it is inevitable that it must become aristocratic: the aristocracy of the socialist bureaucracy. Since individuals in a socialist system pursue their own gain, socialist communalism is faced with tremendous frictions which can only be relieved either by the obliteration of every personal gain and personal preference or by creating and accelerating inflation to accommodate private claims over and above communal claims.

The place of entrepreneurship in society is therefore crucial. If it is placed upon the communal society, socialism is the result. If it is placed upon the individual, the result is market capitalism of an individualistic, competitive nature.

PROF. KIRZNER: I am inclined to agree entirely. There are, of course, a number of distinctions between a socialist society and a capitalist society, including those to which attention has now been drawn. The purpose of the remarks in my paper about socialism was to draw attention to the circumstance that, even within the chosen framework of goals of a socialist system, entrepreneurship within its own framework is a crucially important question, quite apart from the goals to which it would be designed to lead. In his inaugural lecture at Cambridge in 1885, Alfred Marshall considered the possibility of an incentive system which would be based on the Queen's Birthday Honours rather than on monetary profit. Now what should provide the incentives, and what goals are to be considered worthwhile pursuing, is one consideration. Quite another is the impact of an institutional framework upon the likelihood that opportunities (or whatever is to be gained) should be discovered at all. It is to that which I was hoping to draw attention.

DR RALPH HORWITZ (*London Regional Management Centre*): The institutional framework, to which Professor Kirzner refers, is I suggest the *organisation* of the entrepreneur's creative act. This, in business, is the firm. The entrepreneur brings the firm alive but only entrepreneurial management can sustain it in being in the competitive market. This entrepreneurial management contributes three of the four elements of entrepreneurship. Managers who are necessarily entrepreneurial must be creative, initiating and risk-taking, but do not themselves provide capital. The aspect of incentive to which Professor Kirzner has referred is not, I submit, the prospect of reward from ownership.

The incentive to the entrepreneurial manager to innovate and take risks in his own functional job is that his job exists (and expands) only so long as he generates or 'inputs' entrepreneurship into the firm.

For the entrepreneurial manager to become an entrepreneur—a capitalistic owner in his own right—he must have access to capital. I would argue, then, that the major institutional reform to re-invigorate the market economy is a tax reform. Such tax reform would compel the distribution of the total surplus or profits of the firm back to the shareholders in the capital market, so that entrepreneurial managers can have access to capital to break out as entrepreneurs.

Dividend distribution decisions are too important to be left to non-shareholding executives, and plough-back of profits encouraged to fulfil macro-economic investment planning, if entrepreneurship is to flourish.

KIRZNER: I will have to think about this proposed tax reform a little bit. The relationship between the entrepreneurial function and the capitalist function is a long-debated one. Schumpeter used to ridicule the notion that the entrepreneur is the risk-bearer because, he argued, it was always the capitalist who bore the risk, not the entrepreneur. But in real life, the entrepreneurial and capitalist functions are inevitably integrated, although for analytical purposes it is extremely important to separate them from one another. In general, I am strongly inclined to rely on freedom of entry into the capital market to ensure that capital is available to the industries and services where entrepreneurial talent discovers opportunity.

The existence of an opportunity implies access to capital, i.e., the discovery of an opportunity includes the discovery of how to raise the necessary capital. For a man to say: 'I have a brilliant idea but no one is prepared to lend me the capital', means that he has not yet discovered such a brilliant idea. The brilliance of an idea must include the brilliant discovery of how to raise the capital. For that I place a great deal of emphasis on freedom of entry into the capital market. Unless it can be shown that capital markets are in some sinister way blocked against entry, I must remain somewhat sceptical of the reform you propose.

CHAIRMAN: We will now pass from theory to the history of the entrepreneur during the last century, more especially since about 1900.

2. The Entrepreneur in History

LESLIE HANNAH

Director, Business History Unit,
London School of Economics/Imperial College

The Author

LESLIE HANNAH: Director, Business History Unit, London School of Economics/ Imperial College, since 1979. Educated at Manchester Grammar School and St. John's College, Oxford. Formerly Junior Research Fellow in History, St. John's College, Oxford, 1969-73; Lecturer in Economics, University of Essex, 1973-75; Lecturer in Recent British Economic and Social History, University of Cambridge, 1975-78. Author of *The Rise of the Corporate Economy* (1976); (with J. A. Kay) *Concentration in Modern Industry: Theory, Measurement and the UK Experience* (1977); *Electricity Before Nationalisation: A Study of the Development of the Electricity Supply Industry in Britain to 1948* (1979).

I. ECONOMIC HISTORIANS AND ENTREPRENEURIAL OPPORTUNITY: THE INADEQUACY OF THEORY

I suppose we are one brand of the applied entrepreneurial theorists that Professor Kirzner talked about. Economic historians have for a long time wrestled with the problems of why some countries grow at different rates from others; why one country grows faster at some times than at others. I wish I could say that, in the course of their labours, they had produced insights as deep as those of the theorists of the neo-Austrian school. Unfortunately, economic historians have only recently come into contact with this work and the economic theories they have tended to use have had the same shortcomings as those to which Professor Kirzner drew attention. They have tended to omit the element of choice and of entrepreneurial opportunity. The basic framework of analysis (whether it is a Marxist brand of determinism or the technological determinism to which many British economic historians subscribe) leaves little room for spontaneous entrepreneurial creativity. The majority of economic historians working in British universities ignore the element of entrepreneurial opportunity.

Business historians an exception

The exceptions to that generalisation come from the so-called business historians, those who in general look at the lives of individual entrepreneurs or the histories of individual companies. This part of the discipline is, of course, very old. I suppose you can trace it back to people like the muckrakers against Standard Oil in the late 19th century in America, or, in this country, to a rather more favourable public image of the entrepreneur presented by Samuel Smiles in his *Lives of the Engineers* and *Self-Help*.

Writers have been exploring the historical experience of entrepreneurship for a long time and this work has been absorbed into the mainstream of economic history. But everyone will recognise that this early work was tendentious. It was not work which in general gained approbation from the scholarly community, whether it was muckraking or hagiography. Later, there were attempts at Harvard in the 1930s under N. S. B. Gras[1] and, in this country, by T. S. Ashton,[2] to produce more scholarly works. Arguably, however, it was not until Charles Wilson in the 1950s produced a business history of Unilever,[3] which commanded respect from scholars, but which nevertheless got at the heart of the entrepreneurial experience, that the climate changed. His approach was that much beloved by historians—telling history as it is rather than trying to generalise and fit entrepreneurs to the rather inadequate economic theories that we have.

The growth of business history

My comments will therefore be based on the recent work by business historians—men like Wilson and Neil McKendrick[4] in Cambridge, Peter Mathias[5] and Barry Supple[6] in Oxford, Peter Payne[7] and Anthony Slaven[8] in Scotland, and the staff of the Business History Unit which has now been established at the London School of Economics.[9] There has been, in the last few years, an increasing

---

[1] E.g. N. S. B. Gras, *The Massachusetts First National Bank of Boston, 1784-1934,* Cambridge, Mass., 1937.

[2] T. S. Ashton, *An Eighteenth Century Industrialist: Peter Stubs of Warrington,* Manchester, 1939.

[3] C. Wilson, *The History of Unilever: A Study in Economic Growth and Social Change,* Cassell, London, 2 vols., 1954. See also his later *Unilever 1945-1965: Challenge and Response in the Post-War Industrial Revolution,* Cassell, London, 1968.

[4] In numerous scholarly articles on Josiah Wedgwood and in the introductions to the series he founded, *The Europa Library of Business Biography.*

[5] P. Mathias, *Retailing Revolution: A History of Multiple Retailing in the Food Trades based upon the Allied Suppliers Group of Companies,* Longman, London, 1967.

[6] B. Supple, *The Royal Exchange Assurance: A History of British Insurance, 1720-1970,* Cambridge, 1970. See also B. Supple (ed.), *Essays in British Business History,* Clarendon Press, Oxford, 1977.

[7] P. L. Payne, *British Entrepreneurship in the Nineteenth Century,* Macmillan, London, 1974; *Colvilles and the Scottish Steel Industry,* Clarendon Press, Oxford, 1979.

[8] A. Slaven, *The Development of the West of Scotland: 1750-1960,* Routledge and Kegan Paul, London and Boston, 1975.

[9] E.g. G. G. Jones, *The British Government and the Oil Industry,* Macmillan, London, forthcoming, and other books in the series *Studies in Business History.* See also Business History Unit, *First Annual Report 1978/9,* London School of Economics, 1979.

willingness to finance this kind of work in universities, and support has come both from business and from government. Indeed, we have a project starting at the Unit, financed by the Social Science Research Council, to examine the social and educational characteristics of British entrepreneurs over the last century. The obituaries in *The Times* or the entries in the *Dictionary of National Biography* are notoriously inadequate on businessmen, and a multi-volume *Dictionary of Business Biography* is to be published which should do something to redress the balance. More systematic studies of international contrasts in business recruitment and similar questions are also being undertaken in the Unit. I hope that in five years' time we may be able to answer some of the questions which Professor Kirzner has put to this Colloquium.

For the moment, however, I must confine myself to generalisations from the existing work. This research does have serious biases. It has been the case, for example, that most company histories have been commissioned by large corporations, and we know very little about the activities of small company entrepreneurs. This is a very important gap in historical knowledge. There are a few business histories of small firms—for example, by Roy Church on Kenricks[10] and Eric Pasold's autobiographical account of *Ladybird*[11]—but there is very little in the economic literature which gives any impression of the entrepreneurs at the bottom storey, as it were: of the people who start businesses, building them up from scratch, or developing an inherited family firm. The stories are generally those of large corporations, quite simply, the sceptic might remark, because it is the large corporations which in general can afford to commission university professors to write their history.

II. THE LIGHT OF HISTORY

What kind of help can historians give in seeking answers to the questions which are before us today? Professor Kirzner mentioned that one of the avenues of inquiry was the personal and psychological. I am not sure what he had in mind here.

---

[10] R. Church, *Kenricks in Hardware: A Family Business 1791-1966,* David & Charles, Newton Abbot, 1969.

[11] E. Pasold, *Ladybird, Ladybird: a story of private enterprise,* Manchester University Press, 1977.

It seems there are two areas where psychologists have made some contribution. First, there is the analysis of creativity: writers as diverse as Edward de Bono, Wilfred Bion, and Liam Hudson are concerned with what psychological characteristics make entrepreneurs creative, or, for that matter, what makes artists creative. In Kirzner's terms, where does the costless vision, which he places at the heart of the function of entrepreneurship, come from?

Social psychology and 'need achievement'

The second, social psychological approach, is conceptually different. The focus here is usually on what produces entrepreneurial effort: what makes people work hard in order to use whatever creative faculties they have. Certainly the work of McClelland (which one of the previous discussants mentioned), and the work of others in the historical field, has tended to stress this quality of 'need achievement'—the idea that there are some people who, because of childhood trauma, of breast-feeding changes, or whatever, have a strongly internalised need for achivement, which is displayed in profound entrepreneurial effort. It is a sort of post-Freudian son of that old chestnut 'religion and the rise of capitalism'. Yet McClelland's book, *The Achieving Society,*[12] has not in general received a favourable response from historians of the Industrial Revolution, as Mr McKendrick will be telling us.

There have been other attempts to produce testable and plausible hypotheses for more recent periods. There is, for example, a study of American entrepreneurs in the 19th and early 20th centuries which examines their background and particularly their experience of losing a father at an early age.[13] This study reached quite striking conclusions: that many of the successful entrepreneurs in the late 19th century lost their father through death or separation. Now this may be of great interest to economic historians but I wonder whether in a policy-orientated context it leads to very fruitful insights. We have had *dirigiste* governments, but the taste for *dirigisme* must have a limit.

---

[12] D. McClelland, *The Achieving Society,* Princeton, Van Nostrand, 1961.

[13] B. Sarachek, 'American Entrepreneurs and the Horatio Alger Myth', *Journal of Economic History,* Vol. XXXVIII, No. 2, June 1978, pp. 439-56.

Social/educational factors in the British disease

So I will pass from psychology to what seem to be more promising avenues of inquiry among some social and educational factors. There have been some stimulating suggestions in this area in G. C. Allen's Hobart Paper, *The British Disease*,[14] in which he analyses the impact of an anti-entrepreneurial culture on the British view of business and the economy's performance. The central question he asks is whether the public image of business and the general anti-entrepreneurial climate in this country is one which damages recruitment to the managerial and entrepreneurial function, and whether this may be something to do with Britain's 20th-century economic decline.

III. THE CHRONOLOGY OF DECLINE

Before I examine some of the evidence which historians have brought forward on that matter, it would be as well to clarify the view which economic historians have recently developed of the chronology of Britain's economic decline. The national income statistics recently developed by Professor C. Feinstein[15] of the University of York appear to show that, after Britain's impressive 19th-century economic performance, the economy stagnated between 1900 and 1930. Much of the research effort in economic history now goes into trying to explain why the British economic performance in that period was so abysmal and why since then it has improved. That is a more optimistic interpretation than that which most gentlemen on the Clapham omnibus (with their memories of an Edwardian heyday) have. It may or may not be a correct basis on which to start inquiries but it does explain why I shall be paying some attention to that period, 1900 to 1930.

It appears, if you believe the national income statistics, that the so-called Edwardian 'heyday' was in reality the worst period of our economic history, and that the 1930s (that dreadful period of depression) and subsequent decades registered historically respectable rates of growth. The acceleration was not, at least from the 1940s on,

---

[14] Hobart Paper 67, IEA, 1976, 2nd Edition, 1979.

[15] *National Income, Expenditure and Output of the United Kingdom, 1855-1965*, Cambridge University Press, 1972.

as good as that achieved by some foreign countries, but it appears to have been significantly better than the stagnation which occurred between 1900 and 1930.

Missed entrepreneurial opportunities in modern industries

Studies of that period of stagnation have focussed on the question of why the new industries—electricity, electrical engineering, motor cars, and the modern chemical sector—dyestuffs, artificial fertilisers and so on—did not take off into more rapid and sustained growth. The facts are reasonably well accepted. Although this constellation of industries was growing between 1900 and 1930, it was not growing as fast in Britain as in America and Germany. And when you study the attempts to set up companies in these leading sector industries, you usually find that there were relatively few British people involved in trying to set them up in Britain. The role of the immigrant or of the foreign company is large, and the hypothesis which inevitably suggests itself is that native British entrepreneurs did not see this opportunity, or that for some reason—guesses among historians vary from factors such as inadequate education in the sciences to the prestige which business has in society generally—Germans and Americans were much better at doing it.

There is a school of economic history[16] which takes an ostrich-like view of these events, claiming that entrepreneurs were faced with factor prices which prevented them doing any better, that for reasons beyond their control the economy was predestined to decline. But their arguments have generally lacked conviction, not least because the models of profit-maximisation from which their conclusions are deduced are precisely those models which Professor Kirzner has condemned as reducing the entrepreneur to the level of arithmetician.

Apart from this theoretical weakness, the studies often depend on assertions which often simply will not tally with the facts. Take the size-of-markets hypothesis: that America must grow faster than Britain because it benefits from large market size. Apart from obvious empirical objections about some of the more rapid post-war growths coming in countries starting off with smaller markets than Britain's, and the international boundaries of markets, it is not even the case

---

[16] The *locus classicus* is D. N. McCloskey and L. Sandberg, 'From Damnation to Redemption: Judgements on the Late Victorian Entrepreneur', *Explorations in Economic History*, Vol. 9, 1971.

that when British entrepreneurs have had the opportunities they have always exploited them.

The example of electrical engineering: foreign success, British neglect

Take the electrical engineering industry, an enormous growth market. Britain was a bigger market than America for electricity in the late 19th-century because we were highly urbanised and we had a relatively unequal distribution of wealth and income.

At first, of course, electricity was a luxury used only for lighting the houses of the top 5 per cent of the population, so England had the advantage of a large luxury market at the top end. Electricity was later used for street lighting and tramways—both urban phenomena —and England was the most highly urbanised country in the world.

So the British market was potentially bigger than any other world market; the entrepreneurial opportunity was greater than anywhere else in the world. Yet the large companies set up in the electrical engineering industry in this period were British Westinghouse, British Thomson-Houston (subsidiaries of American corporations), and Siemens (a German company). The only British-domiciled company in the top four electrical engineering firms by 1914 was the General Electric Company (nothing to do with the US company of the same name), whose chairman, Lord Hirst of Witton, though by then a staunch supporter of the Empire and the Conservative Party, was by origin a Bavarian Jewish immigrant to this country in the 1880s. There is no doubt at all that, at least in this area of new opportunity, the native Britons in this period left a lot to be desired.[17]

Early success of the British motor industry the 'classical exception'

There are, of course, exceptions, and the classical exception— which Neil McKendrick will perhaps be telling us about since I see he has the biographies of William Morris and Herbert Austin on his desk—is the motor-car industry. Here British entrepreneurs did produce some impressive efforts. No-one has yet been able to explain why. We can all make guesses of the kind that Professor Allen makes in his *Hobart Paper*.[18]

I can back up some of those ideas by my own oral history ex-

---

[17] A more general discussion is in Leslie Hannah (ed.), *Management Strategy and Business Development*, Macmillan, London, 1976.

[18] *The British Disease, op. cit.*

periments in Cambridge. I spent some time casually interviewing professors of science and professors of engineering about their departments' practice of student recruitment in the 1920s and 1930s. The general principle in Cambridge seems to have been that, if you were a good scientist you were told to read chemistry and physics, and if you were a bad scientist you were told to read engineering and go into industry. If you asked the same questions in Cambridge, Massachusetts, I would not be surprised to find that their best people would be going to MIT to read engineering.

The prestige of pure science—an Achilles heel?

I am unable to produce anything more than that kind of hearsay evidence for the moment, but it inevitably strikes one that there might be something in the view that, for example, the reason why British universities have such a high level of productivity—the reason, for example, why we get many more Nobel Prizes per unit of research input than America, France, Germany, Russia or Japan—is something to do with the prestige of pure science which was revealed among Cambridge professors.

Yet the uncomfortable suspicion remains that the price which we have had to pay for excellence in universities—in terms of the opportunity cost of their personnel—has been high. This is not, of course, to say that all university professors would make good businessmen (though wartime experience suggests they would not have been as incompetent as popular mythology might suppose!), but it does suggest that recruitment to business careers might have fallen victim to anti-entrepreneurial bias and a less than optimal configuration of social prejudice, of which universities have been the fortunate beneficiaries.

IV. THE CORPORATE ENTREPRENEUR?

Examples of successful and unsuccessful entrepreneurship and possible causes could be multiplied, but before concluding my paper I would like to raise a second issue which seems to me to be an important one for us to confront at this conference. This is the issue of whether the entrepreneur can take a corporate form; whether it is possible for a corporation to act collectively in the form that an individual entrepreneur is supposed to act.

I am not here going to raise the ugly Galbraithian head, which I know will be very firmly slapped down by one of the later speakers [Sir Frank McFadzean[19] was in the audience—ED.]. But the evidence that economic historians have come up with about 20th-century developments shows quite conclusively that the top one hundred corporations have been very substantially increasing their share of the market—that a larger share of economic activity is now generated within the large corporate sector.

It may, of course, be that this development does not make any difference. It may be that Professor Kirzner's comments on socialism do not apply to the large corporation, that the problems a socialist bureaucracy confronts do not apply to a large corporate bureaucracy. But if we examine recent American work in business history, and particularly what is probably the most influential book on business history written since the war—I am referring to Professor Alfred D. Chandler's *The Visible Hand*[20]—we find a view that is more sustainable than that of Galbraith.

Has the bureaucrat's 'visible hand' overtaken the market's 'invisible hand'?

Chandler argues that the great change which occurred in American industry from the 1860s onwards was to substitute bureaucratic for market forms of co-ordination. He suggests that the visible hand of the bureaucrat in the large corporation became more efficient than the invisible hand of the market at the job of co-ordinating economic activity. This is not crude Galbraithianism; it is an attempt to suggest that the real entrepreneurial contribution, the real opportunity which became available a hundred or so years ago and has become more important since, has been (to use the terminology of Professor Kirzner) the capacity of the entrepreneur to create an arithmetic machine.

This argument may simply be dismissed as Lange's comments on socialism and planning[21] in another garb, but Chandler is able to show that, in large areas of economic activity, the corporation was

---

[19] Author of *The Economics of John Kenneth Galbraith: A Study in Fantasy*, Centre for Policy Studies, London, 1977.

[20] The Belknap Press, Harvard, Cambridge, Mass., 1977.

[21] Essay No. 1, page 19 and footnote 9.

supplanting the market. The theme he suggests as one which economic historians should concentrate on in future does appear to raise the general question of whether the corporation can be an entrepreneur in an important form. It is probable that future work in business history will also have an important contribution to make in this area.

Empirical Evidence Confounds Ignorance and Hostility

NEIL MCKENDRICK

University of Cambridge

The Author

NEIL MCKENDRICK: Lecturer in English Economic History, University of Cambridge, since 1964. Educated at the University of Kent at Canterbury. Consultant Editor for Europa Publications. Author of *Josiah Wedgwood, 1730-1795* (1975); *Thomas Bentley, 1730-1780* (1975). Contributed to *Essays in Economic History* (1962); *Rise of Capitalism* (1966); *Changing Perspectives in the History of Science* (1973). Edited *Historical Perspectives: Studies in English Thought and Society* (1974).

Arthur Seldon: *Dr Neil McKendrick has a habit of writing long prefaces, even longer than mine, but they are remarkably good as self-contained appraisals of the content of the books, four of which he has edited now, and he has 12 more to come. These books are compulsory—I mean compulsive—or perhaps I should say both! And all economists ought to have read them before they dilate on the economics of the entrepreneur.*

In this company, Arthur Seldon told me, you can afford to offer a commercial. Why didn't I say a little about what I was doing both in my own work and in editing the Europa Library of Business Biographies—a kind of Life of the Entrepreneur to match the 19th-century engineers? So I will say a little about the series and what it is trying to do. The first four volumes have appeared, with introductions that are indecently corpulent—of about 50 pages—by myself. The intention of the series is to provide some of the necessary empirical evidence with which one can test some of the theoretical insights offered by our economic colleagues.

Business historians feel there is a vast empirical vacuum. There simply is not sufficient evidence to answer the interesting questions raised by the economic theorists. Let me give you an example of the psychometric approach, mentioned by Leslie Hannah, that is, the idea that one could measure need-achievement, as suggested by Professor McClelland, or Everett Hagen's view of a kind of status re-orientation through economic success. Both of these approaches had a strong impact on business historians and on economic historians in general. They claimed one could explain an event like the English Industrial Revolution in terms of personality change, which could be measured. This notion was very exciting because it said one could apply something like Maslow's 'hierarchy of human needs' to the historical context, and thus explain the sudden emergence of highly motivated entrepreneurs in the 18th century.

Historical evidence conflicts with psychological/sociological theories
But alas, when one examined what they said, fascinating though it was as sociology and psychology, the empirical evidence simply

did not support it. For instance, the whole of this debate, which had reverberations throughout the whole subject, rested on a sample of 72 British entrepreneurs, and the explanation was held to be that the Methodist Revival in the 18th century led to an increase in the supply of entrepreneurial excellence. But of the 72 industrialists listed, nobody could discover the religious beliefs of 29; of a further 21, it had to be deduced through the presence or otherwise of a statue of them put up in their local churchyard, which often owed more to local pride than to ethical beliefs. The result was one found that the famous Methodist Revival, as an apparent explanation of the Industrial Revolution, did not withstand detailed examination of the evidence. Indeed, only two of these entrepreneurs were Methodists; the theory rather collapsed under this empirical assault.

That is a crude example of the need for information, but in the light of the Schumpeterian view of the creative destroyer, the Harvey Liebenstein view of the entrepreneur as a gap filler, or Arthur Cole's claim that the entrepreneur stood as a central figure in the study of economics, welcome and entirely delightful though it is to hear these things, one feels that a lot more evidence is required to test it. What business historians are doing increasingly is to try to provide the detailed evidence by which one can offer some yardstick to judge the performances of the individual entrepreneurs they are studying and test the theories put forward by their theoretical colleagues in economics.

Evaluating the importance of empirical discovery

The difficulty is considerable. When an historian studies an individual entrepreneur, as I studied Josiah Wedgwood, he frequently makes claims about his achievements and finds there is no contemporary measure by which to judge them. If one finds that he conducted a brilliantly sustained advertising campaign; that he used remarkably sophisticated techniques for promoting and marketing his goods; that he used inertia-selling techniques and self-service; that he used 'money-back-if-not-satisfied' policies; that he used market segmentation or product differentiation, and one suggests that that is remarkable, the historian is not in a position to judge how remarkable, or how typical, it is because of the lack of supporting evidence. And I have found that colleagues are naturally sceptical: the tendency among academics when one tells them of a discovery is, first, to say: 'It's not true', and then, when it has been proved, to say: 'Well, we knew it all along, but it's not important because it's not typical'. The problem at the moment is to judge the typicality, the importance, or the characteristic quality of many of these pieces of individual research that the historians are producing.

What the Europa Library of Business Biographies is attempting to do is, first, to provide some of this empirical evidence. The first four biographies have appeared, and there are another 12 in the pipeline. We are hoping to cover not only major figures like Austin and Morris, who have been mentioned here, and Sir Alfred Jones and the Vickers Brothers, who have been published. There are also volumes coming on Courtauld, Lever and so on. We are also planning to cover some minor entrepreneurs because we think it most important to see what they achieved: figures like Newbury, the publisher, and Bentley, the potter. Equally, we want to cover some failures because I believe the historian's concentration on successful entrepreneurs very often makes it seem to the generality of the reading public that success is automatic. We do not have enough knowledge of failures; we do not sufficiently study the bankrupts. When we discuss the successful entrepreneurs, we fail to realise that they were operating in an environment which was frequently steeped in failure. It is very important to emphasise that there is failure as well as success.

I would very much like to have some hostile biographies. This may seem odd for someone who is promoting the idea of entrepreneurial importance. Yet it seems to me that in the English historiographical tradition we have far too bland an acceptance of the entrepreneur by people who study him, and a complete dismissal of him by the rest of society. This contrasts with America, where there is a powerful school of critical attack—I do not merely mean the muckraking school but the attacks by Myers or Moody or Josephson, all of whom had great influence on making historians approach the businessman's rôle critically.

Acceptable face of capitalism?

We are also trying to establish an adequate vocabulary of praise for the entrepreneur, some method by which one can present him in an acceptable light. The unacceptable face of capitalism is well known; the acceptable face, we feel, not so. Indeed, there is not even an acceptable vocabulary of description. It is fascinating for the historian to observe how the businessman in the 17th century was put forward as a 'projector', and then, when he was satirised in contemporary literature, that was rapidly dropped and he became known as either an 'adventurer' or an 'undertaker'. For obvious reasons both those labels were dropped: one was too redolent of risk and dishonesty, the other of death. He then moved on through a whole sequence of names, all of which were rapidly dropped in the search for more negative or neutral names or descriptions. We can all think of 'tycoon' or 'business baron', of 'industrial empires' or 'commercial princes'; all of these have been regarded as unsatisfactory. 'Capitalist' has had unsatisfactory overtones and 'businessman' and 'merchant' have been regarded as too general for the specific, analytical needs of business historians And so he has finally taken refuge under the label of 'entrepreneur'.

Traditional social/literary hostility

We feel that part of this constant search for an acceptable camouflage is explained by the traditional hostility to the businessman in English society. I have tried to explain in my extended introductions to the series of biographies the nature of the characteristically British attitude to the businessman. I have examined our search for a secular ideal, literary Luddism and its reaction to the businessman. And I have studied the enemies of technology and the enemies of enterprise in general and the enemies of the self-made man, and have argued that, in its attitude to business, English society has heeded for too long the Blakeian view that the tigers of wrath are wiser than the horses of instruction.

England has followed its novelists and its poets rather than listen to economists and business historians. Admittedly, when one compares the verbal brilliance of some of the tigers to the honest plodding of most of the horses, it is not difficult to sympathise with their choice. But there is no doubt that anger and dismissive contempt have inspired more memorable prose, more purple passages than have the quieter voices of justification through practical deed. In my view, English society's instinctive response to business and technology has, as a result, been deeply influenced by the view that mills are characteristically dark and satanic; that merchants are the fiends of commerce; and that the businessman's historical rôle has been little more than to serve as a mahout to Dickens's melancholy mad elephants, machines who trampled humanity to death in search of private profit. Invited by Wordsworth to share his just disdain, the majority response in English society has been to accept. Now Blake, Wordsworth and Dickens were not, of course, alone but merely the lead-singers of a whole chorus of disapproval and condemnation.

I have been trying to explain why that characteristic English attitude to industrialists arose. Partly, of course, it is a question of guilt by association with pollution, profit and the inhuman efficiency of the machine. Partly, it is political prejudice. Partly, it can be traced back to anti-semitism or anti-Quakerism, anti-non-conformity or dissent. Partly it is a reflection of the powerful emotions engaged by those supporting the ecology movement and the like; but there is nonetheless an instinctive feeling of disdain for the businessman in England which is reflected in literature, and one of the things I have been trying to do is to look through the English literary tradition to see the way in which the businessman is presented and to try to offer that as some kind of mirror of social attitudes.

I would argue that when the historian is looking for the prevalence of the view that the self-made man is a bounder seeking to grind the faces of the poor, to screw from society the fattest possible profits, he would do well to take note of the accusing resonance which rings from the names of some of our most famous characters: Dickens's Boundaby and Murdle and Gradgrind, Disraeli's Shuffle and Screw, or the doubtful company owned by Meredith's Major Strike, George Eliot's Sir Gavuel Mantrap, Samuel Warren's Sir Sharper Bubble, or Charles Lever's Davenport Dun. Prevailing social attitudes echo all too clearly the condemnation encapsulated in those names. But it is not simply that those names reflect a certain hostility. Very often the literary tradition has done more than that: it has distorted those elements in that tradition which they found emotionally and politically satisfying. They distorted the historical and literary record to suit their case.

Let me give you a single example. Everybody mentions Gradgrind as the archetype of the inhuman, heartless industrialist. If you simply read Dickens, you find, of course, that Gradgrind is a Utilitarian MP and a fat, besotted academic and teacher, but by some curious alchemy he has been turned into a profit-maximising, mechanical, rational, heartless businessman, typical of all who ground the faces of the poor.

Not all writers were hostile to the entrepreneur

Before we become too defensive, we should realise that the assumption that the literary tradition is entirely hostile is simply not true. Donald Coleman, a very distinguished business historian, wrote:

> 'If you look in English literature, if you look for the businessman, you'll either not find him at all or he'll vary from the sinister to the absurd'.

Most historians have assumed that *all* the literary voices are hostile. But it simply is not true. Jane Austen's view of the emergent entrepreneur in Mr Gardner is extremely favourable. Anybody would think that Dickens is wholly hostile to businessmen, but we should remember the Cheruble brothers and the extraordinary picture of benevolence they present; or if you think he's entirely Luddite, remember his admiring view of the engineer Doyce in *Little Dorrit*; and there are dozens of further examples. Had I time, I could take you straight through Blake and Dickens and Disraeli, right up to Lawrence, pointing to a whole series of extraordinary and admiring views. But the critical tradition has presented only the critical voices. That is one warning I would like to make.

Criticism from Right and Left . . .

The second warning I would like to make is against the assumption that all the criticism of the businessman stems from one political direction. There is a comforting suggestion that all the critics are of the Left. This is simply not true. It should be remembered that England did admire its businessmen up to about the 1840s, and the great change in that tradition started with the humanitarian revolt against the appalling conditions suffered in the great slump of 1839-42. In my view, that slump left a more lasting imprint on the literary and historical record than did the slump of the 1930s. But the first voices to leap in and condemn the businessman were the voices of the romantic Right. And remember that the assault on the bourgeois commercial society owes as much to critics from the romantic Right as it does to those of the romantic Left.

. . . especially from female novelists

Let me give a couple of examples of the more extreme denunciations; and note that Mrs Trollope and Mrs Tonna, indeed almost all the early critics of the industrialists, were female: Mrs Stowe, Mrs

Tonna, Mrs Gaskell, Mrs Trollope, all leapt to the attack. You may remember Mrs Trollope's dismissive comment, when she went to America and found that people were proud to be self-made and self-educated, that that simply showed they were ill-educated and ill-made. Her attitude was one of disdainful snobbery to the emerging entrepreneur.

The early attacks on the entrepreneurs incorporated much of the conservative critique, as well as a more radical political stance. For instance, Mrs Trollope's portrait of a mill-owner in her book *Michael Armstrong* ended with a magnificent deathbed scene in which the evil manufacturer, bankrupt both morally and financially, is haunted by all the people he had exploited, maimed or killed; and his wife is left to deliver a marvellous epitaph on him. She says: 'He was an abominable, wicked, low-born, brutal, treacherous, pitiful, cheating,' and, finally, '*manufacturing* savage'. Saving up the word 'manufacturing' as the final telling stroke in her crescendo of hate is typical of this kind of response. Indeed, Mrs Trollope is a perfect proponent of the prelapserian myth, and anybody who studies both the literary tradition and the historical tradition will find that there is in England a curious unholy alliance of the Left and the Right to present the pre-industrial world in order to show, first, that that was a world which should have been conserved, and, secondly, that it should not have gone the way it did in terms of capitalist application; and that the pre-industrial world was a marvellous, golden world in which roses bloomed around the cottage door, everything was delightful, and the organic community predominated. Nothing is further from the truth.

Mrs Tonna and the men of Satan

The other early opponent of those who were to disturb this wonderful Golden Age was, of course, Mrs Tonna. Her bitter attacks on the changing industrial system took the manufacturer and industrialist as the leader in this evil change. Satan took the form of a manufacturer, as one French critic said of her work; and I shall give you one example of what she accused the industrialists of, to show that it was not simply one-way political traffic.

Instead of the old patriarchal relations and the idyllic social scene in which everyone knew his place, suddenly there are factories introducing hot-beds of sedition and false religion. These were mainly non-conformist manufacturers, but nevertheless she said: 'In them the blight of Popery noiselessly spreads'. Souls perish, she said, while their poor bodies are worn out by hard and cruel labour to swell his unholy gains. Sexual evil, we are told, flourished unchecked and was intensified by the heat of the factory rooms, as if the manufacturers were specifically intending to achieve this environment. But worst of all (I won't give you the details of the abominable vices she said were hatched by these monsters), she said that these manufacturers, these new 'millocrats', spread the unutterable curse of socialism (and note that the book was published in 1841), which, she said, was disseminated in their factories by men whom it was hard to think otherwise than as incarnations of Satan. Words almost fail her, but she goes on to say that it would suffice to say that some half-dozen of the young men in the mill become socialists. Beyond that it is impossible to go. Socialism is the *ne plus ultra* of 6,000 years' laborious experience on the part of the great enemy of man. It is the moral Gorgon upon which whosoever can be compelled to look must wither away. It is a doubly denounced world .... Nevertheless, the proponents of this hell, you will discover to your amazement, were the new industrial class.

'The lesser cats of anger'

One of the results of the combination of the conservative, the aesthetic and the socialist critique is to have produced an attitude in the English historical tradition where the businessman has gradually sunk from being taken seriously at all. Indeed, I suggest that today the voice one hears is not that of the tigers of wrath but the lesser cats of anger, constantly nibbling away at his reputation, and that they are the real enemies.

I have an impressive list of examples of the ways in which the industrialist is misrepresented. I have not got time to deal with it here, but I can sum up the basic argument by quoting another fictional hero, Sir Ezra Sterling: 'Prejudice is not just based on ignorance—it depends on it'. In my view the ignorance of the entrepreneur both in the historical and the literary tradition goes a long way to explain the characteristic English disdain for trade and industrialists and businessmen.

Questions and Discussion

ARTHUR SELDON: Our last two vignettes have shown us how the entrepreneur has been viewed, misunderstood and misrepresented for something like a century. That view continues in the works of E. P. Thompson, Eric Hobsbawm and other Marxist historians. We shall now have questions or comments on what is an enormous range of subjects and topics.

CHRISTOPHER TAME (*Historian; Manager, The Alternative Bookshop*): I want to challenge Dr Hannah's thesis based, I presume, on Chandler's book *The Visible Hand*,[1] about the growth of concentration in the American economy to which the book refers. We can counterbalance Chandler's work with that of Professor Gabriel Kolko, who has produced an industry-by-industry study of the American economy at the turn of the century,[2] and has shown that, far from becoming more concentrated and less competitive, American industry was becoming increasingly competitive, and that a number of American businessmen at all levels responded not by becoming increasingly competitive or commercially entrepreneurial themselves. They became political entrepreneurs who called in the state to assist them in resisting competition.

Thus the growth of government was a response to the demands of businessmen to restrict growing competition. This, of course, is not a new phenomenon, as anyone who has read Adam Smith must know.

Perhaps we could see the growth in the changing value structure in America, the growing acceptance of the value of the state and of state interventionism, as giving businessmen more opportunity to utilise the state to prevent competition. There is a changing value structure here. This view is connected with this afternoon's paper on the businessman as hero and villain. A lot of businessmen became political capitalists rather than economic capitalists, political entrepreneurs rather than economic entrepreneurs, which was made possible by a changing social and political environment where government intervention became more acceptable.

DR HANNAH: First, on the issue of concentration. It is very easy to play games on this, and I think John Jewkes does an entertaining hatchet job on Prais's and other estimates of concentration in this respect, in his IEA

---

[1] *Op. cit.*

[2] *The Triumph of Conservatism: A Re-interpretation of American History, 1900-1916*, Free Press of Glencoe, New York, 1963.

Paper.[3] But I do not believe that, if you take the long run, it is possible to say anything other than that concentration has increased enormously. There is no doubt at all that, in both Britain and America, the top 100 firms now control more than 30 per cent of output, nor is there any doubt that in the 1890s it was around 10 per cent in both countries. There have been substantial periods of declining concentration. I believe that in Britain, for example, concentration declined very considerably between 1930 and 1950, but I do not think there is any doubt about the long-run trend.[4]

The question of competition is quite different. I think it is perfectly consistent with the argument that competition has been vastly increased. Kolko analyses concentration data over a very short period at the turn of the century in America, where I would not have any disagreement with him.

On the more general issue of the tendency of entrepreneurs to become political rather than economic entrepreneurs, I would agree with Mr Tame. It seems to me indisputable that this has been one of the 20th-century changes in the nature of entrepreneurship. It may perhaps be possible to take a view of that activity more favourable than the one he was taking. It is arguable that in some areas the capture of the state by entrepreneurs has been desirable. I can think of one case from my own work. The Central Electricity Board, set up in 1927, was one of those rare examples of regulation which produced a real improvement in economic welfare.[5] But it is a matter for empirical investigation whether that is a typical case.

NEIL McKENDRICK: I recently heard a paper by Professor Peter Payne of Aberdeen, who asked the seminar if we could think of any example in which the rôle of political capitalists had been successful, in which decisions taken on political grounds had worked. And we drew attention to the rôle of the electricity industry. Professor Payne countered that by quoting the case of his own research in steel where he has shown the disastrous consequences of public policy and its impact on firms like Colvilles.[6] He made a most eloquent case against political interference, and it was very difficult to offer examples other than the electricity industry to support the alternative case.

---

[3] [*Delusions of Dominance,* Hobart Paper 76, IEA, 1978, which includes, *inter alia,* analysis and commentary on Dr S. J. Prais's research on industrial concentration for the NIESR culminating with his *The Evolution of Giant Firms in Britain,* CUP, London, 1976.—ED.]

[4] L. Hannah and J. A. Kay, *Concentration in Modern Industry,* Macmillan, 1976.

[5] L. Hannah, *Electricity before Nationalisation,* Macmillan, 1979.

[6] [Examined in detail in Part 5 of Professor Payne's *Colvilles and The Scottish Steel Industry,* Clarendon Press, Oxford, 1979.—ED.]

BERNARD POLLECOFF (*Sallek Chemical, S.A.*): I come from the other side of the field, as an employee of an entrepreneur in the chemical industry. The emphasis that has been put upon entrepreneurs as visible top people, visible leaders in companies, puzzles me from my experience in industry. There probably was a time, particularly in an industry like mine, when individuals led companies and were entrepreneurial in style. But it seems that to find the entrepreneur today who is making a success of a company, you need to delve down several layers below the top to find the real decision-makers who are doing the business, which is so constructed that they can make profits for their proprietors.

It would seem that the entrepreneur is the operator within the concern rather than its proprietor, and that very few individual companies are led by their real creative heads. In my segment, the trading element, the contrary is true. The trader is still the creative thinker who looks for opportunities; but within the large corporations I am sure this is no longer so. I think that biographies written about the marketing managers in growth sectors of companies would be more illustrative than the biography of the managing director of the company.

PROF. KIRZNER: I find this observation most interesting. It also connects with a comment made earlier by Dr Hannah about the corporation as entrepreneurial or entrepreneurship in the corporation. A number of rather subtle and complex issues are involved here.

There is a famous paper by Professor Ronald Coase on the theory of the firm,[7] in which he deals with the economic limits to the size of the firm. Some aspects which Dr Hannah discussed might usefully be linked with the issues raised by Coase, namely, that to the extent that the corporation is inconsistent with individual entrepreneurship, this may well be responsible for some of the natural limits to the size of the firm. At the same time, as Mr Pollecoff has pointed out, it does seem to the superficial observer, at least, that entrepreneurship and creativity seem to be exercised by employees of corporate firms. If that is so, it might seem that there is no linkage at all between the corporate form of organisation and possible entrepreneurial limitations on the size of the firm.

Now there are really subtle points here. It was Frank Knight who most cogently pointed out that the notion of an employee as an entrepreneur is almost a contradiction in terms.[8] In one sense, I think Knight was absolutely right. If an employer hires an entrepreneur, clearly it is the employer who is the entrepreneur because he has seen the entrepreneurial quality of the employee rather than the employee himself. If an employee has the alertness to recognise opportunities, but has not had the alertness

---

[7] 'The Nature of the Firm', *Economica*, 1936.

[8] *Risk, Uncertainty and Profit*, Houghton Mifflin, Boston, 1921.

to recognise his own alertness, to that extent he lacks a fundamental entrepreneurship, a point that Knight made very forcefully.

On the other hand, I must agree with Mr Pollecoff that the corporation as an organisation is far more complex than it is often believed to be, since, as Mises pointed out, every individual is an entrepreneur—as is every wage-earner and every consumer. The notion in Mises's *Human Action* is one which encompasses that element of identifying what the opportunities are, before the process of calculated decision-making.

On the question of whether the corporate form of organisation, as other forms of organisation, permits some scope for individual entrepreneurship: there is no reason to believe that entrepreneurship is absent at the lower or middle ranks of the corporation, but what one has to look for is not the notion mentioned by Mr Pollecoff—of the employee finding opportunities to make profit for the employer. If a man finds opportunities to make profit for his employer, he is acting as an employee, not as an entrepreneur. Entrepreneurship consists of finding opportunities to make profit for oneself. To the extent that an employee in a corporation is able to make profit for himself, entrepreneurship can and does exist within the corporation. The extent to which such profit is legitimate, or the particular legitimate forms such profit-making may take, may be quite subtle. There may be, for example, opportunities for advancement, for promotion, for attracting attention in the market at large—these are all more subtle concepts of entrepreneurial profit than the simple pecuniary profit we usually identify with entrepreneurship. There are thus somewhat conflicting elements of entrepreneurship within the corporation.

DR HANNAH: I agree that this is a very important issue. The answer to the problem given by Al Chandler, the American business historian, is that one of the main organisational innovations in the 20th century has been the multi-divisional corporation which has attempted to replicate the workings of the market within the corporation. He argues that the capital market's attempts to work out whether one company is better than another are not very successful. The London capital market, for example, is not terribly good at this task, but the head office of a large corporation is very good at doing it for its own divisions. In a sense what they are doing, Chandler argues, in allocating new capital to their divisions according to their profitability (in terms of the management accounts, not the published accounts) is obtaining the information required for the efficient working of the market. Big companies will survive only if they do indeed replicate the market in this way to achieve the efficiency the market is supposed to achieve but cannot always do so because of imperfections.

This idea links up with what Coase was saying. His article is, indeed, seminal, but I think it draws much too simple a distinction between the firm and the market. It seems to me there is a vast continuum of forms of economic organisation between the firm and the market and not simply a dichotomy in the form he suggests for, no doubt, theoretical convenience. These forms of organisation range from long-term contracts, which are the nearest to the market form, for example, the kind of arrangement that Marks & Spencer has with its suppliers, to the multi-divisional corporation which in some formal sense is like a firm, but can properly be seen as an alliance of quasi-firms. In this structure there may be strong entrepreneurial incentives, of a kind which a socialist mechanism cannot provide, but which nonetheless can be provided for the head of a division by making his remuneration dependent on market response, or on some other understood measure of performance which relates to something other than the views of his superiors, and is in some sense determined by market forces.

Whether big firms are in practice good at such functions (rather than merely being potentially good) is quite a different issue. It may be that, particularly in this country compared with America, we have perhaps too many incentives for the large firms and not enough for the small ones. It is, for example, fairly obvious, both in this country and in America, that the crisis of the 'seventies has been dealt with rather better by small firms than by larger ones, although many of the former have gone bankrupt. If you compare the portfolio of shares in small and medium-sized companies over the 'seventies with a portfolio of large companies, you will see that it is better to have been investing in small companies. For the sceptical I quote in evidence a chart published in *The Economist*[9] showing the 1974-79 differential between AMEX (American Stock Exchange) shares and the New York Stock Exchange shares, broadly an indication of the difference between small and large companies in the US.

ANTHONY HOLLICK (*Research Officer, Alliance of Small Firms and Self-employed People*): I have essentially three questions. First, Neil McKendrick was discussing Maslow's hierarchy concepts and seemed to me to be saying that research had been done in an effort to discover the religious affiliations of businessmen. But I could not understand what relevance this had to Maslow's hierarchy. It does not seem to me that formal religious ideas are in any way contained in Maslow's hierarchy.

NEIL McKENDRICK: I was using shorthand. Historians have increasingly been taking note of work by people like Maslow on the hierarchy of human needs, recognising that the need for achievement, just as for love, for sex or for friendship, or anything else, was an important element

---

[9] Chart accompanying article, entitled 'Why Wall Street Looks Oversold', *Economist*, 20 October, 1979. See also Hannah and Kay, *op. cit.*, pp. 96-7, for the UK experience.

in analysing human behaviour and, in particular, entrepreneurial behaviour.

One of the most important applications of this kind of psychological insight was to try to measure the change in motivation of entrepreneurs through time, which is, I think, a very fruitful and beneficial approach. Where it became distorted and went wrong was in endeavouring to explain the old view of the supremacy of the Protestant ethic in entrepreneurial behaviour. It was misled by the inadequate empirical evidence about the religious beliefs of the leading entrepreneurs of the Industrial Revolution. It assumed they were non-conformist, and therefore that this was the key. When that assumption was subjected to empirical testing, it turned out to be completely erroneous. That is not to say that the psychological approach is not valuable, but simply that here, because historians took for granted information which turned out to be quite wrong, they were led up the wrong path. Indeed, it turned out that among the leading entrepreneurs of the Industrial Revolution there was no disproportionate contribution of Methodists, but there was a very large, disproportionate contribution by other minority groups: the Quakers and the Congregationalists. This discovery, of course, completely upsets the timing and the chronology of McClelland's and Hagen's explanation. But still that is not to say that that kind of psycho-historical approach is not valuable. It is simply that it used the wrong information. I was not criticising Maslow but the nature of the historical evidence available to him.

ANTHONY HOLLICK: Professor Kirzner seemed to me to be saying earlier that an entrepreneur who was unable to obtain the capital resources to pursue his entrepreneurial activities was being insufficiently entrepreneurial, or in effect was not being entrepreneurial at all, since his objectives and his efforts did not take adequate account of the necessity to obtain funds. It has certainly been my experience and that of a number of entrepreneurs that considerable numbers of people in British banking and business (and I understand this is now a phenomenon which occurs on the other side of the Atlantic too) do not seem to be much interested in the creation of new business activity, but are more interested in the re-allocation of existing business activity. Very often they are not interested. It does not matter how apparently good the prospects appear, they are just not interested in dealing with that sort of risk.

PROF. KIRZNER: The idea that capitalists might not be interested in higher returns is one which can be accepted only within rather narrow limits. If, indeed, an entrepreneur finds an opportunity which he believes is sufficiently promising to convince him that it is worthwhile offering a rate of return substantially higher than the going rate, I see no reason why capital should not be forthcoming on that basis.

DR HANNAH: Where someone has an entrepreneurial idea and someone else has capital, it is possible for both to act as entrepreneurs. The category of entrepreneur is not exclusive: an ideas man and a financier can come together and agree to share the benefits of bringing the capital and the idea together. Both are engaged in entrepreneurial acts, which is how I would try to solve the problem raised earlier of whether capital and entrepreneurship are the same thing. I think it is obvious that they have to be brought together, but there are difficulties in this for essentially the same reason that economists come up with theoretical problems in analysing the market in information. It is very difficult to sell an idea. Suppose I have a brilliant scheme to make money on the Stock Market; I can guarantee to make millions of pounds in one day, but I have no money. How do I sell that idea? No one will buy it until they know what it is. But once they know what it is, once I tell them, they will not need to buy it. And yet you have to find some way in which idea and capital can come together, but it is very difficult: whether it involves the head of a company talking to a divisional controller with an idea, and trying to work out how to reward him, or a completely independent entrepreneur going to a bank and asking for money to develop an idea. It is a problem which is at the centre of many innovative business activities, not one for which it is very easy to devise institutional procedures, but one which true entrepreneurs (whether capitalists or ideas-men) are grappling with all the time.

DUNCAN BURN: I am always interested in historical rediscovery. If we take the dates of the developments that have been discussed, we see a rising growth rate at the end of the 19th century, then a slowing-down from 1900 to 1930, and then an upward curve. This is related to something that happened between 1900 and 1930 when Britain was not as quick as America and Germany at industrial innovation.

This was true as long ago as 1851. At the 1851 Exhibition it was said by the Commissioners that England was lacking in the intellectual elements of production. Now if you are going to explain the 1900-30 period, or the current situation, this long history is very important. It was indeed recognised that there were educational deficiencies, and, as I showed in my book on steel,[10] people in the steel industry were complaining that they could not recruit from the universities and regretted the tendency for graduates to go into scientific research or other pursuits. So it is a very old story. This English deficiency certainly relates to the type of person engaged in industry and, of course, it is striking that all the people who made the three great innovations in steel of the 1860s to 1880s in Britain

---

[10] *The Steel Industry 1939-59: A Study in Competition and Planning,* Cambridge University Press, 1961.

came from outside the industry, and all the minor cumulative but fundamental developments came in foreign steel industries—American, German, French, Belgian—but not in the British. I am sure that we must examine this evidence, and not merely study the national income. The drop in the national income from 1900 to 1930 is almost certainly related to the loss of the natural advantages on which we could earlier rely. The coal industry found its domestic market static and its overseas market halved. This, and the fact that subsequently we have gone up much more slowly than others, when technological development was very much faster, is easy to explain. But I do not think it indicates any change in the basic ability we have in our institutions to develop and apply, and to evolve new ideas. It would be a mistake, I think, to interpret the trends in that way.

One of the factors I thought important when I studied the steel industry in particular was the nature of the capital market. Even the large American corporation like General Electric can be regarded as part of a capital market. But if you examine the German capital market you see much more entrepreneurship than in most of the European capital markets.

3. Capitalist Cameos

NIGEL VINSON—**Plastic Coatings Limited**

KEITH WICKENDEN—**European Ferries Limited**

SIR ARTHUR KNIGHT—**Courtaulds Limited**

The Authors

NIGEL VINSON, MVO: started his own company, Plastic Coatings Limited, in a Nissen hut when he was 21. Over the next 18 years he built it up into a public company employing over a thousand people. Two years later, having won the Queen's Award to Industry for Technological Innovation (for its process of applying plastics as paints—but with a drying time of seconds), and numerous Design Council prizes, he sold out to the Imperial Group. On his passport he describes himself as 'Inventor'. He is President of the Industrial Participation Association, Deputy Chairman of the CBI Smaller Firms Council, a Trustee of the IEA, and a director of numerous companies.

KEITH WICKENDEN: Member of Parliament for Dorking, 1979. Chairman of European Ferries since 1972. Educated East Grinstead Grammar School. Partner, Thornton Baker, 1958; Joint Liquidator, Rolls-Royce, 1971.

SIR ARTHUR KNIGHT: Chairman of Courtaulds, 1975-79. Appointed Chairman of the National Enterprise Board, November 1979. Educated at Tottenham County School and the London School of Economics. Joined Courtaulds in 1939, appointed Director in 1958, Financial Director in 1961. Author of *Private Enterprise and Public Intervention: The Courtauld Experience* (1974).

Arthur Seldon: *We now come to real-life capitalists who will give short accounts of a main problem they had to solve—only one, so don't expect them to tell you all their secrets. We shall not know if they are saints or sinners until Donald MacRae tells us after lunch.*

We start with Nigel Vinson, who is by way of being an inventor, as well as an entrepreneur.

Plastic Coatings Limited:
Successful Entrepreneurship based on Inquiry and Invention
NIGEL VINSON

I always had a deep ambition to be self-employed—to be my own boss—or, as I would put it now, to be free of other people's power. After National Service in the Army, I weighed up my prospects and, in place of university, decided to learn about plastics, since I believed that by joining a growth industry I would at least stand a chance of growing with it. Probably this was the only rational decision I took, and a vital one, because the plastics industry has grown at a 14 per cent compound rate for years, enjoying the benefits of both substitutional and absolute growth.

From work-bench to sales office to entrepreneurship
After one year with a company employing 100 people I moved from the bench to the sales office, where I noticed we often received inquiries that we could not fulfil. I approached my boss about setting up a joint company and he advised me to go it alone since 50/50 companies seldom worked. I did—at 21 you have little to lose, and that is an important qualification. Subsequently, over the years, at least six others left me to start their own businesses—a good example of entrepreneurial spin-off.

The two key factors
Premises and the cost of money are *the* two key factors in entrepreneurial success or failure.

It took me six months to find suitable premises and to this day I regard the inadequacy of premises as one of the major handicaps when starting a business. It is partly a consequence of our planning laws which, by enabling redevelopment through compulsory purchase, have largely obliterated those twilight buildings that are the ideal premises in which to start.

Today the acute shortage of risk capital prevents many potentially successful ventures from starting. There appears to be almost unlimited *loan* capital, but it is *risk* equity that entrepreneurs require because they cannot, in the early years, afford the interest payments on loan capital. What is required is a new form of private sponsor—a new form of the rich aunt—sponsors who, unlike the bank manager, are not in danger of losing their jobs if they take too many bad risks: they will merely lose their shirts!

When I started I was fortunate in that Bank Rate was relatively low—because the higher the rate of interest, the more economic pressure on marginal opportunities. Entrepreneurial endeavour is like a pyramid. At the apex one in a hundred will survive if interest rates are at 20 per cent. At the base fifty out of a hundred will survive if interest rates are at 5 per cent.

Price competition, historic and actual costs

The reality is that, whether we like it or not, price competition is based on historic not on actual costs, giving a double hurdle for new ideas to overcome since they, of course, are financed on current costs.

It used to be argued that rising interest rates would take the heat out of the economy; if so, the converse remains true that lowering them will put the heat in again.

Whatever the argument about the negative rate of interest and real return, the fact remains that if the arithmetic constantly keeps the price of money above the cost at which people can sensibly borrow and make a return, it will gradually shrivel up entrepreneurial endeavour and thus destroy the regenerative process.

Self-financing business

I was particularly lucky to choose a self-financing type of business that processed its product within 30 days and turned its capital over every six months, because such a cash flow is vital when starting up.

It is not surprising that most of the success stories today have been in retailing—for precisely this reason.

I also learnt two truths—that no cash-flow plan survives contact with reality, and that budget guesses should not be given the authority of facts.

Companies today have one advantage: they can write off 100 per cent of investment annually. They have, effectively, depreciation at choice or what is sometimes misleadingly known as 'free depreciation'. There is, of course, nothing *free* in such accelerated amortisation, but this method of write off (a return to 18th-century cash book accounting) is vital to the growth company, big or small.

The gift of self-criticism

Apart from good health, entrepreneurs have to be egotistical. When you start up everybody thinks you must be mad or others would be having a go at the same thing. So you need an unproven self-confidence in your ability, and a blissful ignorance of the problems you are likely to encounter, allied to a determination to overcome every obstacle. Having started, you need essentially the ability of self-criticism, to learn from your mistakes, to kick your own backside, because nobody else will. Only those who have been successful in the world's eyes know how thin, in reality, is the margin of success over failure. Above all, success is seldom due to just one lucky choice, it is a compound of hundreds of little quarter per cents of attention to detail.

At the end of the first year I employed 3 people, at the end of the second 11, then the third 30, and the company grew to 1,000 employees over the next 17 years at a 20 per cent compound rate of growth of turnover. Productivity increased over this period by a factor of at least 900 per cent. The company has tripled in size since I left it.

I had no formal training other than in the Army, so I suppose I worked on the principle of taking one's decisions intuitively and then backing them up factually.

Simple, effective ideas and small units

The reality is that good inventions and good ideas do not necessarily have to be complicated and expensive to be effective. Barbed wire transformed agriculture, the polythene bag made deep freezing feasible, and the chain saw revolutionised timber felling. These relatively simple inventions, requiring no great research programme, have had far more impact on society than carbon fibre or the hovercraft.

In business you need both the trade winds with you and the ability to be a frigate amongst the galleons—but it is not so much *what* you do as *how* you do it. All business is essentially a question of man management and sharing of problems. From an early date we deliberately split our company into units never exceeding 300 people, and even then the most productive employed approximately 100. We used a comb structure, each part independent but held together by a strong central spine of services. I tried to run the company on common-sense grounds, practising the simple belief of treating others as you would wish to be treated yourself, and following the age-old naval maxim of walking the ship—of being seen.

At flotation approximately 10 per cent of the shares were taken up by the staff, both with their own money and with what I gave them by way of a 'thank you' for all they had done for me.

As chairman of a public company you have power and prestige but you are not a free man. The job should be totally time-consuming. So, having been lucky enough to achieve at 39 what most men strive to achieve by 60, I decided to sell out while I still controlled 55 per cent of the company. I am now a 'wiz kid' turned 'was kid', with multiple interests.

The major obstacles to small enterprise

To return to the major hurdles in starting a business: First, premises. The chief difficulties arise from government controls over the natural workings of the market. Our planning regulations when applied to small companies are far too onerous. Local authorities already have the power to waive some building regulations and should be encouraged to do so, particularly where unrealistic enforcement would inhibit employment opportunities.

I would also like to see the law amended so that people could conduct businesses in their homes, provided they did not create a manifest nuisance—if they did their neighbours could sue under common law. Such an amendment would enable people to start businesses in their own garages and encourage enterprising wives to do dressmaking legitimately in their front parlours. It is in such humble ways that many businesses start. As is well said: 'Inside every moonlighter there is a small businessman trying to get out'.

Then there is the cost of borrowing. Other highly successful trading nations have recognised that companies with negative cash flow are in a very different position from those that have self-generated resources. Unlike established companies, new enterprises cannot offset start-up losses against other profits. There is, therefore, a fundamental difference, and that is why compensating concessions are necessary. We shelter our children—we should not be ashamed to protect our industrial seedcorn.

The American model—the Small Business Administration

In America they have solved this pump-priming problem by allowing investment companies with special tax concessions. I think their Small Business Administration model is one we could well follow. At the same time, the government should introduce a simple tax amendment that would enable, say, 80 per cent of capital losses in *bona fide* small enterprises to be offset against personal income. This would bring back a new form of the old rich aunt and that personal investor interest that is so badly needed.

The small enterprise, labour relations and economic reality

To finish on a more philosophical note. Apart from the more obvious justifications for small businesses—economic vitality, dispersed initiative, disseminated economic power, sources of invention, etc.—there is one equally, if not more, important justification: man's need to belong, the need to know that his contribution really counts. The smaller company satisfies this need, as most have a naturally participative atmosphere—as the labour record of this sector proves.

What is more, in the smaller company the employee is not insulated from the consequences of his own behaviour. He is more in touch with economic reality, and is not this, above all, what is wanted on the labour scene today?

Nobody would suggest that there is not a sensible role for both large and small companies in our industrial spectrum, but I hope that my few words will give added support to the theme of this conference which is, I believe, that the industrial forest regenerates from the bottom, and that we must cherish our seedlings.

Arthur Seldon: *That is one kind of capitalist who has a genius for invention. Our second is of a different kind. I always regard him as our sea-borne Freddie Laker, although I gather he is now thinking of other ventures, too. I think his story is worthy of a long book—or, at least, a short one. He is going to tell a story that ought to be far more widely known.*

European Ferries Limited:
Idea into Action—an Unsolved Problem
KEITH WICKENDEN

First, I think I should say that I sit here as a complete and utter fraud, because earlier today we heard from Professor Kirzner that to be an entrepreneur one needs to be making money for oneself— that is an essential element. Since I spend the whole of my working life devoting myself to the interests of my 90,000 shareholders and do not do so for myself I most certainly, on that interpretation, am not an entrepreneur. You will note I say my working life is devoted to my shareholders—that indicates perhaps that what goes on at Westminster is more in the nature of high comedy than work!

The second reason I am here on a fraudulent basis stems from the introduction to this part of today's proceedings, which tells us that we have to give you an account of problems we have had to face and how we have solved them. The problem I want to describe to you has not been solved. But since it is capable of being solved and it undoubtedly *will* be solved, perhaps I am not altogether fraudulent on that aspect.

An untapped market . . .

My company, as some of you may know—because I suspect there are some half-price shareholders here—is primarily in the business of transporting people, cars and commercial goods across the Channel to the Continent of Europe. We have been reasonably successful in doing that—but there is a very considerable market that we have not been able to tap. That is the market of the passenger who wishes to travel to the Continent without his car. To our shame and our disappointment that class of passenger—and about 7 million of them went through Dover last year—is still largely carried by our competitors. The reason they can carry them is that our competitors are owned by the British Railways Board and they are able to offer that which we cannot offer: a city centre to city centre through service. We have tried with coaches and the like but it is not the same as being able to get on a train at Victoria and get off a train at Paris. This is a gap in our marketing.

. . . and a possible solution

In addition, for the short-haul passenger (London-Paris is a perfect example), conventional air methods mean that one is spending about three times as much time actually getting to the airport as one is spending in the air. That is another problem that needs to be solved. So when we were approached three or four years ago by a starry-eyed romantic who wanted to build airships we did not treat his idea with quite the scepticism with which everybody else has treated it ever since. Because, as we all knew and as we know now, airships have flown successfuly in the past. The Germans operated a transatlantic service before the war. The only problem with airships at that time was, first, that aerodynamically they were not all that stable, and, second, that they had a distressing habit of bursting into flames and killing everybody on board, which has perhaps prejudiced people against them! Both these problems can now, however, easily be solved: the second because airships need no longer be filled with hydrogen but are now filled with helium, which is inert, and the first because a great deal more is known about aerodynamics now than was known in the 1930s and earlier.

So when we were approached by the starry-eyed enthusiast who wanted us to finance the building of a saucer-shaped airship, we took the idea very seriously indeed. So did other people, although sadly they dropped out on the way. A major mining company was very interested in it since there are apparently a number of mines around the world which are not economically viable because of the cost of providing the infrastructure to get the product out and the employees in—that is a problem helicopters can solve only to a limited extent.

Airships, if they could be operated successfully, could solve it even better.

We have examined this project very closely. We believe that all the answers have been provided to the many questions which were posed and that now we should be ready to go. But here I came up against a fundamental objection from many of my shareholders: not that they thought that the project would not work or indeed that it would not be successful, but that we as an operating company should not be involving ourselves in manufacture. And I think that is probably a fair comment because we do not really know much about manufacture, particularly aerospace manufacture. Freddie Laker, for example, buys his aircraft, he does not build them.

Nevertheless we have been able to persuade our major shareholders that we should provide a substantial proportion of the research and development money which is required—perhaps up to a half, provided other investors could be persuaded to put up the other half. And this is where we have so far run into some difficulties. In July 1979 we had a public flotation in an effort to raise the other 50 per cent of the money—perhaps we did not handle it very well, perhaps our advice was not as good as it ought to have been—I do not know. I know that there were 350 applications for shares, not one of which came from a financial institution or company. They all came from enthusiastic individuals. So the issue was a failure.

We are now rejigging it and doing it in a different way and there will hopefully shortly be another issue. If that one fails the project will go to the Continent of Europe where we have offers of money on the table right now. I hope that will not be necessary.

Criteria of success in entrepreneurship

To turn then from that project to a few general remarks about entrepreneurship. I have been listening to this word entrepreneurship all morning—I am not sure in fact that there is such a word. But as I am talking about airships, why should we not talk about entrepreneurship? I think there are two particular factors in being a successful entrepreneur.

First of all, one needs to be slightly nutty, because you have to look at things from a rather different angle from most people. I am quite sure that when Nigel Vinson started to build his company he was told by everybody that he could not possibly succeed, and it was the fact that he refused to accept the advice of eminent accountants, lawyers, bankers and everybody else that he did succeed.

Secondly, you need a great deal of luck—and not only do you need a great deal of luck, you need the type of mentality that turns bad luck into success. It is not always appreciated how often what appears on the face of it to be a disaster can be turned to one's advantage. Again I believe it is the sort of mind which immediately starts to examine how difficulties can be turned into opportunities that provides entrepreneurial skill.

Gaining a competitive advantage

Perhaps I can give you an example. About 12 or 13 years ago—I cannot remember exactly when it was except that it was during one of Britain's recurring economic crises—Mr Roy Jenkins, the then Chancellor of the Exchequer, at the beginning of January, slapped stiff exchange control on people taking their holidays abroad. At that time my company was quite small (we were operating only one or perhaps two ships), and this decision came right at the height of our passenger booking season. Now it was not so much that the £50 limit—it seems an absurd limit now, looking back at it—was unreasonable. If you took the average family going abroad, £200 at that time was more than they spent anyway. It was the psychological belief that people were going to run out of money and be stranded abroad.

My predecessor's first reaction was one of horror: the bookings for the coming year on which all our cash-flow forecasts had been based would disappear. By the time he got to his office he had dreamed up a scheme by which our passengers would be able to purchase what we called Townsend vouchers. In other words, we are one of the very few companies which has printed its own money— we printed vouchers up to a limit of £30 per passenger which our customers could buy at the same time as they bought their tickets. They could spend them on board on these ridiculously underpriced duty free goods which you know we sell. The effect was, first, that we were offering something that our competitors were not; secondly, and more importantly, I think, we were removing the psychological barrier which many passengers might otherwise have felt. I think it says much for the Bank of England that they gave Exchange Control permission for this scheme within four hours of being asked for it. And great credit to them for that.

There was another rub-off effect and that is that in our balance sheet we still have a provision for £30,000 worth of vouchers that have never been cashed for some reason which I do not understand. So it was a very good thing all round. That is one small illustration of a way in which what could have been a disaster to a small company on a very tight cash budget at that time turned into a great success. It gave us a considerable marketing advantage over our competitors.

'Having a nose for business'

The other area of entrepreneurship I would like to take up—and Nigel Vinson put it rather more elegantly than I would have done: he said it was taking one's decisions intuitively—having a nose for business. This is something that in my view cannot be acquired—it is something some businessmen have and some have not. I always remember, when I was in practice as an accountant, I acted in the Midlands for a builder who probably left school at twelve. He was certainly a man of no formal academic training at all, but a very successful builder, and a very good one. When we went in to produce his accounts every year, as firms of accountants always do we put in half a dozen highly educated young chartered accountants for about 8 weeks to produce his accounts. At the end of this process I would go to see him with the figures they had produced and I would say: 'Well now, Mr Bloggs, you've had quite a good year, you've made £118,674'. And he would say: 'Really? I made it £116,278'. And to this day I have never found out how he did it—but he was always within £5,000. He was a natural businessman—and one can think of others.

As I say, it is not something which can be acquired—either people have it or they have not; people take wrong decisions on the face of it which turn out to be right and those are always the great decisions. You can take a decision for what appears to be all the right reasons and it may turn out to be utterly disastrous. My own company did that some seven years ago when we bought a small cargo airline in the belief that this was merely an extension of our cargo business by sea and could easily be welded in. Something which we would readily understand and have no difficulty in building up. What we had not appreciated was how different the economics of airlines are to shipping lines and that we simply had not got the technical expertise to run this business successfully. In practice it was a dismal failure.

On the other hand—and I may add that we had every business study in the world on that company before we bought it but the decision was nevertheless wrong—we had a rather more successful enterprise when, against the advice of all our professional advisers, we decided to bid for a dock in competition with a nationalised industry. Mind you, we made a mistake in that as well because we thought it was a commercial decision and it turned out to be a highly political one. That one was successful because our instinct was right. It was certainly a good company and our instinct that we could battle against the politicians and even the government and win also turned out to be correct, although I think that owed more to the House of Lords than to any inherent brilliance on our part.

So there we are. All I have done is just give you a very short cameo, as I have been asked, of one problem which we are trying to solve and which we shall solve even if we have to take it to the Continent of Europe. And, secondly, just a few disjointed thoughts on what may or may not make a successful entrepreneur.

Arthur Seldon: *Our third capitalist is again different. He is not so much one who built a new firm, but one who saved it at a period of dire crisis. He is an economist; he was an evening student in the late 1930s; and like me he learned some of his economics from Lionel Robbins, and also from the late Arnold Plant, who would have graced this venue. Since then our paths have diverged; he is now chairman of a great company. I am an employee; I work at, or at least I am paid by, a great Institute.*

Courtaulds Limited:
Encouraging Entrepreneurial Behaviour in a Big Company

SIR ARTHUR KNIGHT

The briefing from Arthur Seldon asked for accounts from entrepreneurs of the main problem they had had to solve and how they solved it. As applied to myself some would question the applicability of the word 'entrepreneur'. For example, in the early days of the Manchester Business School two or three of us on the Council were trying to take seriously Oliver Franks's vision of the School as a partnership between industry and the academic world, and were behaving in ways which the academics regarded as inappropriate for so-called lay members. I saw a letter from the Director referring to 'the bureaucrats of big business'. I was clearly one of those he was writing about.

More encouraging was the man into whose business our pension fund had invested quite a substantial sum. I was finance director at the time and very much involved in that particular decision. The man running that business into which we had put our investment said a few years later, when things were going well, that he and his colleagues wondered at times how I had brought myself to be so bold as to invest that amount of money in a new and untried business, and had come to the conclusion that I must be an entrepreneur at heart and wanted to prove it to myself before it was too late! That was some 15 years ago.

The temptation, faced with Arthur Seldon's brief, is to think about the individual projects with which one has been associated personally—their initiation, the assessments, the decision process, the unexpected, both favourable and unfavourable, and the persistence or abandonment leading to successes or failures. But most of the individual projects which I could identify as mine go back into the past—twenty years or so ago. The issues which they raise are now very familiar to me and, I guess, to those who have looked at individual project analysis and management. So that, if I were to take any one of these as my theme it would lead to a predictable statement and to some predictable questions and responses. I fear we would all be confirmed in our preconceived attitudes.

The elements of entrepreneurial behaviour

So it seemed to me much more interesting to look at the period since 1975 when I became chairman and to ask what I have done that could be called entrepreneurial, leaving aside those specific projects which, as chairman, I have got involved in by way of probing, testing, showing support and so on—projects which other people will identify as essentially theirs. The more directly personal activity in these last four years relates to the ways in which it is possible in a large business to develop entrepreneurial behaviour. For that purpose one needs to be clear about what one regards as the elements of entrepreneurial behaviour. As I see it there are seven:

first, taking initiatives;

second, assessing the factors in the situation;

third, the decision process;

fourth, finding the resources;

fifth, the accidents of circumstances which either help or hinder;

sixth, the activity which makes the decision come true if that is at all possible;

and, finally, the rewards which go with success and the penalties which go with failure.

To analyse these entrepreneurial factors in the context of a large business is unfashionable—'small is beautiful'—but industrially the next decade in this country is going to be determined for good or ill by the performance of the large businesses. The top 400 account for something like 80 per cent of our total industrial production. The time-scales during which these companies grow or decline are not short. I once saw a report that 10 of the top 50 disappear from the list in every decade. I suppose in the context of the time it takes to build up and establish a business, that is a fairly rapid rate of turn-over. But, given that that is the time-scale, I think it justifies my assertion that over the next decade it is the performance of the big companies that we should most concern ourselves with—important though it is to foster the small and to recognise that it is the small of today, or a few of them, which will become the large of tomorrow.

In 1975 I suppose my chief realisation was that I was succeeding a man who by any tests was an outstanding entrepreneur. Indeed, Professor Donald Coleman, in the third volume of the Courtaulds history, which will be published in 1980, gives a fascinating analysis of the man in those terms. Now my position, as I saw it, was different in two ways. First, I could not as an individual hope to behave in a company as large and diverse as Courtaulds in the ways that my predecessor had. I have described the way in which he did the job in a book published seven or eight years ago and therefore need not go into that sort of detail now. The second factor was that, as I saw it, the conditions in which we were having to operate were changing rapidly and those methods, whatever their past success, were not going to be appropriate to the future.

Policies to encourage the spirit of entrepreneurship

The actions which seemed desirable in order to ensure a widespread entrepreneurial spirit were five in number:

(i) *Unwind 'verticalisation'*

To unwind what had become known as 'verticalisation'. Verticalisation was a recognition of the advantages to be gained from being manufacturers of textile raw materials, transformers of these into intermediate products, and manufacturers of final products for the consumer market.

Substantial success had come in the preceding several years by exploiting this vertical chain in two specific boom situations. Basic capacity decisions were taken at the centre, managers at what was called the 'sharp end' were looked upon to sell and to get the best price for the products. Transfer prices were generally adjusted (as it was put) to take the profit at the 'blunt end'. This meant that, for most general managers, the profit and loss account of the business for which they were responsible was determined primarily by decisions which were not theirs. A number of the raw material suppliers had begun to take their in-house customer too much for granted. So in some respects quality, product development and so on received too little attention. And, at the using end, the managers had a first-class alibi: whatever went wrong could so often be ascribed to failures on the part of the in-house supplier.

So in those days my colleagues and I decided that the in-house users of raw material should not be bound to buy all of their needs internally but should be actively encouraged to seek outside supplies. It took a little while for the outside suppliers to accept that there was a real change of policy and that they could regard these Courtaulds users as genuine customers and not merely as probing in order to get useful information to be deployed against them. But we have persisted.

At times it looked an expensive process, and there was criticism about my allowing the users to buy from outside competitors at a time when the in-house plants were working well below capacity. Profits of some magnitude appeared to be being lost. The process was a difficult one. The apparent cost was transitory. We took the view that, in time, with persistence, the in-house supplier would become the preferred supplier because in terms of price, availability, service and so on, they could become the better performers. We have not got there yet. But I feel that a great improvement has been made.

(ii) *Identification by market and technology*

The second major change was to recognise that if managers were going to feel a sense of responsibility they must have a clearer notion of the kind of business they were working for. Each business is identified by reference to its markets and its technologies. The management talents which are required are widely different as between raw material supplier and a consumer products supplier, essentially because of these differing market characteristics and technologies. A regrouping of the business into product groups was therefore carried out, so that the skills and talents appropriate to fibres on the one side, to fabrics on the other, to consumer products on the other, should become the tools of the trade for all the individuals in the management of activities within their particular product group.

(iii) *Filling a gap—marketing expertise*

The third element in this process was to recognise that past success had been based on the high quality of the technical and production people who had been brought into the business. More than half of the general managers had come into the business through the research route and had been transferred from there into general management—and very able people they are. But the changing market scene meant that their background and their training had not always given them quite the marketing emphasis that was called for. So we brought in from outside talent of the kind which we hoped would fill a gap and provide these general managers with the service and the support needed to fill this gap in their own training and background.

(iv) *Marketing plans*

Fourth, as a direct consequence of this managers were asked to produce marketing plans, looking three years or so ahead.

(v) *Cultivating the customer*

Finally, it was necessary to be seen to be cultivating the customer, to get over by example that the customer is the important person.

*   *   *

The brief required me not only to describe the chief problem but also to say how I have solved it. My problem has not been solved. It never will be. I believe there has been a major change in attitude and approach. I believe it is a management approach which is more suited to the conditions in which we have to operate. I believe it is recognised in the market-place. But the trading results so far are pretty unencouraging and I can only console myself that, but for these changes, the results could be much worse than they are.

The general managers are there because generally they are the best people. You cannot, despite some of those who write about business, and talk about it, suddenly go to the market-place and find large numbers of trained, able, alternative managers. Most businesses have to spend time seeing what can be done to achieve the best performance with the best of people who are available. All I could claim in the case I am describing is a limited move in the right direction.

Can big business offer sufficient incentive?
Penalties for failure severe . . .

If I turn back to my seven criteria of entrepreneurial behaviour and ask myself how far I think it possible in the large company to produce the conditions for entrepreneurial behaviour, I would hesitate most about the last. I would hesitate most about whether the rewards for success or the penalties for failure are sufficient to generate the behaviour required for adequate performance. The penalties for failure are much more painful than is sometimes realised. Certainly in my talks with senior civil servants I am very conscious that they have no sense of the extent to which at times in a career in business one is knowingly putting one's career at risk and that the penalty for failure could be, not just the end of that career with that company, but considerable uncertainty about what the next career would be. In my experience each large group does develop its own way of going on so that the individual has got a large invested capital in having learned how things get done in that group. The skills do not necessarily translate, and I have noticed that those who try to make the translation later in life—say, after the age of 40—very often find it difficult. So there is a sense of being at risk which is far beyond the consciousness, the experience, of those who have done well in other fields of activity.

. . . but rewards cannot match those of
old-style entrepreneurship

I turn now to the rewards side of the equation. It is difficult to offer anything like the potential rewards that people can gain for themselves in independent business. The independent man who is successful, or who fails, is so in large degree because there are elements of good or bad luck and these are well-recognised by those who are observing the scene closely. In a large group, therefore, the rewards must bear some relation to an objective assessment of the circumstances, because it is impossible to design the system to provide to a sufficient extent those large rewards or large penalties which depend on luck. But I do not think that the disparities of the past are necessary to get people's full commitment and endeavour. Donald Coleman in I think his first volume of the Courtauld's history describes a period (1871-80) when Sam Courtauld was taking £46,000 a year out of the business and had a total income of some

£70,000. The foreman dyer was paid £62 10s per annum and the average earnings of operators were £15.

In my experience you do not need disparities as wide as that to get good performance. The disparities have to be there. People are not going to devote themselves to preparing for and handling these demanding situations unless there is some visible preferred treatment. But I think we sometimes exaggerate the extent to which the prospect of enormous material reward is the only spur to action.

My final point is to suggest that we are not looking at bureaucrats on the one side and entrepreneurs on the other. We are looking at ways in which we can encourage more entrepreneurial behaviour than we get, within the framework which the big company can offer. Whatever we think of that framework we are going as a practical matter to have to live with it for quite a long time to come.

Questions and Discussion

SIR LESLIE SMITH (*BOC International Ltd*): It seems to be more difficult for our capital market to finance entrepreneurial activity than it is for our competitors, particularly Japan and the USA. The Japanese capital market works to a longer time-scale, and much of the activity in the USA has been spun-off from their huge defence expenditure. What, then, is the panel's view of the attempts by the NEB to fill the gap in the UK?

SIR ARTHUR KNIGHT: The time-scales of innovation tend to be longer than the capital market normally finds acceptable. The outstanding example is Rolls-Royce aero engines, with its 15-years time-scale for a new product; and in the situation in which we find ourselves, this requires nationalisation if we are going to have it at all. Its American competitors have always kept their government's support in different ways, and this factor has to be borne in mind. The time-scales the big investors envisage are, I think, very often too short in Britain because we have an over-developed Stock Exchange. One reason for this over-development is the nature of our tax system, which has led people to look for capital gains; this in turn has led to shopping around for shares instead of looking for income. This has therefore put pressure on all who are running businesses to look for short-term rather than long-term performance.

To move away from the situation in which we are into something better would require the big investors to take a very different approach to their investments. There has been considerable pressure on them in the recent two-year discussions as a result of the Harold Wilson Committee and alternative notions from the TUC which they found unpopular, but I have not yet seen any sign of an alternative. There is a real problem, and so I think I would answer Leslie Smith's question by saying there has to be an NEB because of it. I do not, however, agree with him that it has got to be based on a large armaments industry. One must remember, after all, that in the late 'fifties and 'sixties we did take a wrong turning, with the 'white-hot technological revolution'. It was based upon notions in central government about what should be encouraged. This meant that all of our best young engineers were enticed into aircraft, aerospace and military electronics. As Freeman of the University of Sussex has pointed out, these were the very areas where, because of market size, the Americans were bound to succeed, and in that very period the best of the Germans were going into mechanical engineering and other civil-directed activities. I would, therefore, be very hesitant about putting as much emphasis as Leslie does on wanting to see the source of this coming from an armaments decision—until we get a European basis for our defence, which is miles away.

NIGEL VINSON: In terms of entrepreneurial endeavour, it seems odd that there is a wisdom in the NEB (in investing funds) that is not to be found in the General Electric Company which has £800 million of cash. What prevents GEC from going into the area in which they are most knowledgeable? They are either unadventurous and the NEB is therefore right, or GEC are right and the NEB is wrong. We shall have to wait and see.

M. T. J. WALLIS (*Midland Bank*): I should like to deny the suggestion just made that it is the NEB, and the NEB alone, which these days provides risk finance, venture finance, 'start-up' finance. There has been a significant change over the last two to three years in the demand from the small business in particular—the small business market-place—which is now beginning to result in a response from the major financial organisations.

If I speak of my own bank it is simply because I am more familiar with it. During the last two or three years we have set up a cluster of investment companies, some of which exist to provide our own money, that is, bank money, as risk capital for smaller start-up operations. Some exist to provide money brought forth partly by ourselves, partly by pension funds and other institutions. This money is available in tranches from as little as £5,000 up to the multi-million pound investment. It is 100 per cent risk capital, which we put in the form (Mr Vinson made this point) of equity capital. Interestingly, if we have had a disappointment it is that the entrepreneur, particularly the smaller businessman, is emotionally reluctant to part with any portion of his ownership or to participate in profit-sharing with us. That is the biggest single impediment to our investments we have experienced so far.

KEITH WICKENDEN: Perhaps I should ally myself to those remarks. I believe the National Enterprise Board is doomed to failure because by its very nature it is dependent on the whims of politicians. If there is one certain thing in life it is that you should never allow political decisions to interfere with business decisions. The National Enterprise Board is bound to become merely an agency which spends government money on propping up industries in order to save jobs. I very much doubt whether we shall see any significant investment by the NEB in new industry, which would require an entrepreneurial attitude. It is highly significant that the one industry which the NEB claims so much credit for is the micro-chip industry. But if we had any sense at all we would invest in the software industry. It is a far larger market than the micro-chip industry but it is not so glamorous in political terms.

PROF. CHARLES ROWLEY (*University of Newcastle upon Tyne*): As I understand the process of entrepreneurship, the entrepreneur is the principal catalyst in what Joseph Schumpeter would have said was the process of 'creative destruction'. Sir Arthur Knight spoke about the importance of the large company over the next decade. This would seem to me within the British context to pose major problems. Within the large corporation in Britain both management and labour are opposed to this process of creative destruction to the point where it is very difficult for entrepreneurs to be successful.

Let me briefly cite the case which seems to typify this problem, namely, the technology change at Times Newspapers. It was quite clear from an early date that the best process of adjusting and introducing that change was to disband the existing organisation and to start from scratch. But it was in the interests both of management and of labour to protract the conflict, ending up almost certainly with manning levels very little different from the original, with incomes much higher and with limitations on the use of the new technology. This can be a real problem in a labour market within a large corporation, where both management and labour are resistant to change of the kind upon which an entrepreneur is entirely dependent.

SIR ARTHUR KNIGHT: This is in the nature of the job that some of us have and these are the problems we must deal with. The whole point of entering into this discussion is to get it more widely accepted that these things are capable of being dealt with, that the job of management is there and must be fulfilled, that it is possible to make changes. If we were to accept Professor Rowley's statement as an assertion of what the future holds, then it is a gloomy prospect indeed, but a number of us are active in seeing what we can do about it.

PROF. WALTER ELKAN (*Brunel University*): Must we not distinguish quite sharply between the nature and 'qualifications' of entrepreneurship in large firms and in small ones? It is true that a few entrepreneurs move from small to large—Mr Vinson, for example—but the gifts required by Sir Arthur Knight as Chairman of Courtaulds are not the same as those required by someone who, for example, recognises that there is money to be made from helping investors to buy old stamps.

I suspect ('hypothesise', as some would say!) that very few people become entrepreneurs of *either* kind who have not seen the exercise of entrepreneurship in others at close quarters—among their own family or close friends. Usually they have grown up in an entrepreneurial environment which removes some of the fear of acting on entrepreneurial hunches. Let me give an example. In the mid-1960s it was obvious to me that there was a good deal of money to be made in Durham, where I was then living, from starting a University Bookshop, but I did not do it. The man who did was, like me, 'foreign' to Durham and a professional (school teacher). Unlike me, a second-generation 'professional', he had been brought up by parents who ran an antique shop. Taking risks was familiar to him.

If my hypothesis is well founded, there might be, at first sight, some danger for the perpetuation of entrepreneurship in the growing concentration of industry, and the growing size of firms, which economises on the demand for entrepreneurs. But that is probably true only superficially. The growing concentration is mainly in manufacturing industry—business comprises many other activities. Nor is the concentration of production necessarily incompatible with the growth, or survival, of the number of small firms, so that quite large numbers may continue to grow up in or alongside a business environment.

What is more worrying is that so few who come to take a university degree have grown up in such an environment. A disproportionate number have parents who are professionals or, if they work for businesses, do so in a managerial rather than an entrepreneurial capacity. This may be a further ingredient in the explanation why few graduates end up as entrepreneurs. Even that may be changing, as witness the mushrooming of new firms in both the hardware and software sides of micro-processing. But notice how many of them have spent time in the USA and *seen* entrepreneurship pay off.

RUSSELL LEWIS (*Daily Mail*): I want to raise what I think is the most worrying question about the British economy: the difficulty of managers becoming capitalist entrepreneurs on their own account. The British

Institute of Management recently showed that in the last ten years British managers have managed on balance to save nothing (I am not speaking of the highest level of management—the sort of person who might break out and go into business on his own account), while their equivalents in Germany or France have managed to save in the last ten years a hundred or a hundred and fifty thousand pounds.

In America in the micro-chip industry, a classic example of people becoming tycoons out of quite small enterprises, Silicon Valley is full of people who have created large enterprises out of practically nothing. This raises two questions. One is that we need to change the tax system—and it does take time, after all, to change taxes—but more than this, as Nigel Vinson emphasised, we have to remove the obstacles that prevent people from starting in a small way. I mean our planning regulations seem to make it very difficult for anyone to set up, for instance, in a garage in a residential area. He is forced to go somewhere where his overheads will be high, in a factory, perhaps; and so starting up becomes almost impossible. This is particularly relevant to the micro-chip industry because the real opportunities are in assembly. Big firms can make the chips for assembly though one does not really need much capital at all—just a screwdriver and a soldering iron. If the state leaves you free to get on with it in your garage, there's a chance it might be the start of something which could grow into a very big industry. These are the sort of obstacles which prevent the small enterprise getting off the ground.

PROF. KIRZNER: I would like to present a brief reaction to the fascinating accounts by the distinguished business leaders we heard earlier. It seemed to me as I listened to them that they confirmed my guess that the charge they had been given was somewhat inaccurate. The charge was to describe the main problems they had to solve, and how they solved them. My guess, which was confirmed, had been that the most arresting aspect of what we were to hear was that the entrepreneur's rôle was filled not by solving any perceived problems but by placing themselves in the position where problems raised and presented themselves.

The entrepreneur's rôle is never to solve a problem once it has been perceived; it is always to be present, to have placed himself in the position where he will be able successfully to solve the problems which arise later on. This was confirmed by a reference made by several of our speakers to the rôle of luck. The rôle of luck in entrepreneurial profit is a fascinating, exceedingly subtle one, over which I have agonised a great deal. It seems to me that the entrepreneurial function is fulfilled to a large extent by placing oneself in precisely that position where the good luck will fall.

4. The Entrepreneur in the Private and Public Sectors

SIR FRANK McFADZEAN

Chairman, Rolls-Royce Limited

The Author

SIR FRANK MCFADZEAN: Appointed Chairman of Rolls-Royce, 1980; Director of Beecham and Shell; Chairman, British Airways, 1976-79; Chairman, 'Shell' Transport & Trading, 1966-76. Visiting Professor of Economics, University of Strathclyde, 1967-76. Educated at Glasgow University and the London School of Economics. Author of *Galbraith and the Planners* (1968); *Energy in the Seventies* (1971); *The Operation of Multi-National Enterprises* (1971); *The Economics of John Kenneth Galbraith: a study in fantasy* (1977).

Arthur Seldon: *Sir Frank McFadzean has special claims to sit on this platform. First, he is an entrepreneur as well as an economist; secondly, he has been an entrepreneur, or at least the head of enterprises, in both the public and private sectors. I asked him to discuss the similarities and differences between the role of the entrepreneur in these two sectors.*

I. THE DEVELOPMENT OF ENTREPRENEURSHIP

Words such as entrepreneur or entrepreneurial ability, flair, thrust or alertness are freely used but seldom defined—probably because of the difficulty in doing so. The original entrepreneur deployed his own resources with a view to earning profits, either by meeting a known consumer requirement or by stimulating a demand for products new to the market in which he operated. He did not always succeed but the basic aim was there. As technology developed, and ventures increased both in size and risk, organisations evolved to mobilise resources beyond those in possession of a single person. Individual proprietorships were supplemented by partnerships and joint stock companies. Writing in the period of pre-industrial capitalism, Adam Smith expressed a preference for partnerships over corporations since management and capital ownership are in the same hands; as a consequence more 'anxious vigilance' will be displayed in the supervision of the business than will be the case in a joint stock company where management is largely divorced from the ownership of capital.

As usual Smith's argument has force; but anxious vigilance cannot of course be equated with entrepreneurship—indeed a surfeit of it could well paralyse the will to take any risks at all. Entrepreneurship involves a journey into areas of varying uncertainty and if, as the early Taoist philosophers so elegantly expressed it, there is a bright side to the hill, there is also a dark side; the possibility of success carries with it the risk of failure, and the hope of profit, the fear of loss. It is a widespread belief, without any empirical evidence to support it, that entrepreneurship is more aggressively pursued in the single proprietor/partnership/small company sector of the economy than in that of large corporations.

Indeed, to give the impression that the smaller units are the go-go element, they are sometimes referred to as 'entrepreneurial' corporations to contrast them with 'mature' corporations, a phrase partly coined to give a geriatric overtone to the larger units in the economy.[1] It is not necessary for our purpose today to examine all the mythology that has flourished from this artificial distinction. Suffice it to say that those who propound this view accept that entrepreneurial corporations seek to maximise their profits as required by the theory of the market, but, since the prime aim of the management of mature corporations is their own survival, they will conduct their affairs to produce only the level of profit necessary to keep the shareholders quiet and make themselves independent of the capital market; as a consequence they will always opt for a low-risk, low-return project in preference to a high-risk, high-return venture.

Romantic and naïve assessment

All this is a romantic and rather naïve assessment of how the economy operates. There are aggressive entrepreneurs among the smaller business units, but there are others which have taken few risks since their act of foundation. There are small businesses in the retail trade, road haulage, mechanical engineering and foundry industries, where the conduct of operations has scarcely changed over the decades. For every Wolfson and Gulliver, for every Thorn and Weinstock, there are hundreds of small enterprises which jog along with little alteration over time in product range or manufacturing and distribution methods. Technically entrepreneurs, they display little sign of entrepreneurial thrust. They have no desire to push beyond their present horizons; within this constraint they perform their necessary function in a modest fashion.

And the same is of course true of some large companies, although it is doubtful if these are quite as numerous as the politicians who prattle on endlessly about the regeneration of British industry would have us believe. The validity of criticism depends on the calibre and credentials of the critics. For example, in the early 1970s a 'whizz kid' criticised the management of Scottish Metropolitan Property on the ground that it had failed to follow the trendy finance pattern which subsequently helped to precipitate the secondary banking

---

[1] J. K. Galbraith, *The New Industrial State*, Hamish Hamilton, 1967; Penguin Books, 1969.

crisis. In the sequel the 'caution' which was criticised as ultra conservatism did more for the shareholders than the flamboyance of some of the company's competitors.

II. RISKS V. GAMBLING—A TWILIGHT ZONE

Indeed, at the more thrustful end of the market there is, irrespective of the size of the units involved, a twilight zone in which it is difficult to define where entrepreneurship ceases and outright gambling begins. Many ventures leave room for considerable and genuine differences of opinion about risks and viability—in a well-run corporation these are freely debated—and it is often only possible to evaluate particular decisions after—sometimes long after—the event. The obsession of some groups of economists with the measurable frequently results in the importance of the immeasurable being overlooked; and the flat-footed, often single-figure trend prognostications of the armies of witch doctors and soothsayers obscure the fact that, in the real economy where decisions are made, assessments of future prospects, and hence the present-day value of given investments, vary widely. In practice they vary so widely that some large corporations seem to take risks which others assess as being beyond the bounds of reason.

Failures and crises

The spectacular failures and crises are well known and some are well documented: Burmah, Curtis Wright, Rolls-Royce and the RB-211 jet engine, General Dynamics and the Convair 880 and 990, Concorde (which by the end of 1978 had cost Britain and France together some £1,584 million, with some £200 million still in the pipeline), British Leyland, British Steel, Chrysler Motors, Olin Mathieson and Montgomery Ward—but there are many more. Shell's incursion into the High Temperature Gas-Cooled Atomic Reactor might have had a far-reaching effect on the Group if the management had not set about cutting its losses vigorously once the initial error had been realised. The medical scanner of Electrical and Musical Industries, hailed, and rightly so, as a great technological achievement when it was produced, is now proving a heavy cash burden. Imperial Group's bid of $28 per share (against a pre-bid market price of $15·25) for

Howard Johnson has been greeted by one section of opinion as a thoroughly bad deal and by another as a sound long-term strategic decision, particularly if sterling should resume a downward trend. Dalgety's bid for Spillers has been variously greeted as putting an albatross around its neck and affording a golden opportunity for revitalising a conservatively operated business.

In the examples given—it is possible to find more almost every day in the press—some of the errors of judgement, which always become visible with the effluxion of time, could have been foreseen and avoided at the outset; the adverse effects of others could have been modified by more speedy action as the mistakes began to manifest themselves; but the final assessment on the quality of still others will have to be reserved for some years to come.

Size in entrepreneurship

Vigorous entrepreneurial pursuits are not the prerogative of the smaller units in the economy, nor is ultra-conservatism to be found only in large corporations. Nor is there any proof at all that high-risk, high-return projects will be rejected by the managements of big concerns in favour of low-risk, low-return investments. The basic nature of certain industries even precludes a choice between the two. In the exploration for crude oil the stakes are high, and the odds against success of single ventures, particularly in wild-cat areas, are substantial but, when effort is crowned by the finding of an oilfield, the rewards can be massive. Any corporation, mature or otherwise, behaving in this industry as Galbraith and his followers suggest, would never leave the launching pad.

Again some activities, such as the production, liquefaction, transportation and reception of natural gas, involve such substantial sums of money—some schemes cost over £1,000 million—that only large corporations can undertake them. It is absurd to suggest that the pushing forward of technological horizons which has taken place in the natural gas industry is not entrepreneurial merely because it is conducted by large corporations. Moreover there is no conflict, as is sometimes implied, between survival and maximisation of profit. The two are inter-related. Of course in a highly uncertain world any corporation, irrespective of size, should weigh up the risks of particular investments and the possible consequences of a failure of judgement. To refrain from doing so is not being entrepreneurial— it is being stupid and irresponsible.

Cost-reduction—entrepreneurial or not?

Recently one of Galbraith's disciples mocked cost-reduction investments as not being entrepreneurial but merely enhancing 'the security of the technocracy in an absolutely safe way'. It is, of course, correct to say that cost-saving investments enhance the security of the particular technocracy which makes them but they equally undermine the security of all other technocracies that fail to follow suit. In established industries with little or no growth, entrepreneurship is largely in cost-reduction investments—devising new means of producing the same things more cheaply. In practice it usually takes the form of gaining a cost/time advantage over competitors. The companies which deployed the first giant tankers had the edge over their rivals until they too followed suit; the companies which invested in secondary processing capacity to upgrade the end-products of crude oil refining will have an advantage over their competitors until they also invest in the necessary plant.

It has to be recognised, however, that being first does not always secure an advantage; the second generation of VLCC's (Very Large Crude Carriers) and jet airliners, for example, were superior to the trail-blazing equipment. The economic penalty which would normally flow against those first in the field from such improved technology has, however, been cushioned by inflation. This is in no way to argue in favour of inflation, merely to record that some business decisions might not have looked so robust in its absence.

III. PROBLEMS OF ENTREPRENEURSHIP

Entrepreneurial alertness

In his interesting analysis Professor Kirzner laid great emphasis on entrepreneurial alertness and, of course, this is a pre-requisite; it is a highly important component, which is often under-estimated, in the total process. All of us in this room take the telephone for granted as a useful, almost necessary, instrument. It would seem exaggerated to suggest that its potential required much in the way of entrepreneurial alertness; yet three years after Alexander Graham Bell's breakthrough one of the top technical advisers to the Post Office, Sir William Preece, himself a distinguished engineer, viewed the telephone as an amusing toy and assured the Society of Telegraph Engineers that there was no place for it in England.

> 'Here', he observed, 'we have no difficulty getting servants if we pay them, but the difficulty in America is to get "buttons" at any price to run about for you as in England . . . I have [a telephone] in my office but more for show as I do not use it . . . If I want to send a message to another room I use a sounder or employ a boy to take it'.[2]

Again, the current issue of *The World Economy* quotes a letter from the Governor of New York to President Andrew Jackson on a new form of transportation known as 'railroads':

> 'As you may well know, Mr President, . . . carriages are pulled at the enormous speed of 15 miles per hour by "engines" which in addition to endangering life and limb of passengers, roar and snort their way through the countryside, setting fire to crops, scaring the livestock and frightening women and children. The Almighty certainly never intended that people should travel at such breakneck speed'.[3]

Today it all seems like voices from another planet—but it was real enough at the time. Identification of opportunities is therefore essential but the entrepreneurial process is only completed when the opportunities are seized and developed. This implementation requires an ability and a courage to take risks, which are not necessary in the identification of the original opportunity.

Delegation and administration

Here we come up against another problem of entrepreneurship. Some of the characteristics which can launch a venture successfully—stubborn perseverance in the face of scepticism, the single-minded determination that overcomes the impediments to the introduction of something new, and personal domination of all aspects of a project—can be the same characteristics that run a business into the ground when it has grown to a size beyond the detailed control of a single individual. Henry Ford is a spectacular example, but there are many more.

At quite an early stage in the growth cycle of a business, entrepreneurial thrust has to be supplemented by good administration,

---

[2] Presidential Address to the Society of Telegraph Engineers, 1893.

[3] *World Economy*, Vol. 2, No. 3, 1979, p. 342.

much of it of a routine nature. Bills have to be presented and paid, accounts must be maintained to certain minimum standards, tax returns submitted and management information developed; legal advice has to be available and personnel records and policies established. As a business expands, so does its administrative content. A substantial business staffed entirely by entrepreneurial talent would probably fail to meet the minimum necessary administrative and accounting standards; *per contra*, if it were staffed entirely by administrators it would, sooner or later, wither on the vine. A balance is necessary but the larger the organisation the more important it is to ensure that the atmosphere is conducive, and receptive, to new ideas and that the systems are sufficiently flexible to reward the innovators.

Influence of chance

Again, it has to be accepted that chance can play a substantial rôle in human affairs and particularly in business. In discussing this with the late Lord Thomson of Fleet, he readily accepted that this factor had exerted a considerable influence in the content and shape of the group he had created during his life but stoutly argued that, if an individual had the basic ability to seize opportunities, sooner or later one would be identified. Thus, while chance can shape the nature of the final destiny, it is the ability to seize it that ensures that there is any destiny at all.

IV. ASSESSMENT AND CALCULATION

Now the amount of assessment and calculation embodied in the entrepreneurial process varies widely. The cockney barrow boy who sallied across the Channel to buy candles because of an imminent power strike—he was subjected to the moral disapproval of a non-entrepreneurial television commentator for the substantial profit he made as a consequence—probably acted on nothing more than a hunch that candles must be cheaper in France, where the electricity supply looked secure, compared with Great Britain, where it was under threat. At the other extreme, a large corporation which acted on hunch alone would soon spin out of managerial control.

Entrepreneurial decision-making

Here my views are somewhat at variance with those of Professor Kirzner. He argued that the task of calculation leading to the final decision is itself non-entrepreneurial, but this is only true in a purely mechanical sense; the figures and probabilities used in the calculations have an appreciable entrepreneurial content. The information for most decisions starts off in the market-place with research into customer requirements and the probable future trend of their preferences; it involves the assessment of

- the probable total market, the strengths, weaknesses and possible intentions of competitors;
- the probable trend of the corporation's own product volumes, costs and possible prices;
- the probable sources of funds and the amounts available for investment and dividends;
- the changes in technology and the additional capital required to meet the projected demand at the lowest possible cost;
- the political climate in which the business will be allowed to operate and the possible major discontinuities that could arise.

The ultimate objective of the total activity is to try to arrange the affairs of the enterprise so as to produce the maximum return on its investments. Here again this is not always achieved in practice but the aim remains—and it is common ground between a private sector group such as Shell and a public sector corporation such as British Airways. And it is equally common ground that uncertainty cannot be eliminated, nor the future forecast with any great degree of accuracy.

Operating a business requires the exercise of continuous judgement on the constantly changing alternatives, including the opportunities that have passed unnoticed, and the flow of new information that could well dictate a change of direction. Nor is it correct to assume in this process that the decision-makers know precisely what it is that they do *not* know. The designers of the Comet aircraft did not appreciate the significance of their lack of knowledge of metal fatigue, any more than did the first builders and owners of the large oil tankers understand that forcing water through a nozzle could produce sufficient static electricity to ignite an explosion if the gas mixture was in the critical range.

Indeed, in major entrepreneurial decisions, particularly when high technology is involved, it is prudent to take into account what can be called the Murphy factor. This embraces not only a healthy respect for Murphy's law—'what can go wrong will go wrong'; it also makes allowance for the now accepted fact that Murphy was of an optimistic disposition.

V. CAN NATIONALISED INDUSTRIES BEHAVE ENTREPRENEURIALLY?

It is not easy to fit nationalised industries into an entrepreneurial context since nobody is clear what the purpose of nationalisation is. It is a subject in which logic and objective analysis have played an insignificant and seldom visible rôle; they have been crowded off the stage by the vote motive, political hysteria degenerating at times to near gibberish and endless compromises to maintain the unity of the Labour Party. In the mythology of state ownership, it is postulated that 'the people' own the nationalised industries and it is to them that managements are accountable. In my few years with British Airways 'the people' for these purposes consisted of four different Secretaries of State (they succeeded each other with remarkable rapidity), three Permanent Secretaries, and one appearance before the House of Commons Select Committee on Nationalised Industries. They were all estimable citizens but hardly constituted the people of Socialist folk-lore.

Again, references to the market economy as 'a jungle' and high-sounding phrases about 'commanding heights' and 'producing to serve the public and not for profit' send the zealots into ecstasies at the annual conference and at the hustings; yet the slogans all beg the basic question of how, in the absence of a market economy and the price mechanism, it is possible to determine the types and quantities of goods the public wish to purchase.

Vagueness of objectives . . .

Some of the emotional and irrational elements in nationalisation were highlighted when in 1945 the Government admitted that it had no clear idea of the objectives which should be set the management of the newly taken over coal industry. This basic problem was loftily dismissed by stating that

> 'the precise criteria which should be applied to measure efficiency . . . is a subject which should repay thought and some of us are thinking about it'.[4]

This is the equivalent of seizing someone else's motor-car without knowing how the steering wheel, brakes, clutch, and accelerator operate but assuring everyone, as you drive off, that such matters will repay some thought and somewhere along the way you will think about them. Thus hand in glove with the increased politicisation of power came the increased amateurisation of large segments of the economy.

. . . and arbitrary political interventions

Grafted on to this vagueness about objectives were the often arbitrary interventions of politicians. Negotiations on basic subjects, such as wages and conditions of service, were taken out of the hands of some managements and many were required to take action clearly inimical to the economic viability of their corporations but justified by a vague appeal to 'the national interest'—increasingly a euphemism for the vote motive. Here again, Adam Smith was right when he remarked that he had found little good stem from people who paraded this particular affectation.

The 1967 White Paper on the financial and economic objectives of the nationalised industries represented an attempt to take the problems out of the realm of political rhetoric. Future investment proposals were to be justified by present-day value calculations using a test rate of discount of 8 per cent—raised in 1969 to 10 per cent. Where nationalisation had eliminated competition—and it is necessary to remember that many of the criticisms levelled at the industries are due to the exercise of monopoly powers rather than the ownership of the equity—prices should not only cover purely accounting costs but should be reasonably related to costs at the margin—precisely the argument for resource allocation through the market economy. Having justified the nationalisation of several industries because of the supposed inadequacies of the market economy, the search for reality in their operation eventually forced the government

---

[4] John Jewkes, *The New Ordeal by Planning*, Macmillan, 1968, p. 98.

to instruct the Boards to conduct their affairs as they would have done if they had not been nationalised. Unintentionally, the White Paper served to highlight how fraudulent and counterfeit had been the icons, endlessly paraded for the veneration of 'the people' by the High Priests of State Ownership.

Intervention again—price freezing

But the new realism did not last long. In yet another futile attempt to avoid the inflationary consequences of its fiscal and monetary policies, the Government froze prices in several nationalised industries; the managements were once more set adrift on a sea which afforded few navigational aids. Too many politicians are insensitive to the consequences of arbitrary interventions of this type, particularly the repercussions on management motivation and union attitudes when subsidies are substituted for price adjustments.

Open-ended access to the public purse, which was the inevitable result of this policy, produces, sooner or later, a breakdown in financial discipline; if a surfeit of Adam Smith's 'anxious vigilance' can paralyse risk taking, a deficiency can speedily produce a 'rake's progress'.

Currently the nationalised steel industry is making losses which, even in the fatness of these pursey times, can only be described as massive, but such has been the deterioration in financial discipline that there is still resistance to the closure of uneconomic plants, and few seem to see anything incongruous any longer in the trade unions advancing wage demands which can only widen the yawning gap between the high cost of the input and the lower value of the outturn.

When, in many cases, it is not even possible to allocate responsibility for success or failure, it might seem unduly subtle to try to assess the presence or absence of entrepreneurial characteristics in the nationalised industries. Indeed it can be argued that many of the managements were never given a sufficiently clear mandate or the necessary authority to show their mettle. The endless political tinkering, to further interests other than the interests of the corporations concerned, must always have an adverse effect on management and performance.

In fairness, there has been a growing awareness of this dilemma in both political parties. By the end of 1978, for example, it had been established that British Airways would be permitted to rationalise its fleet with the aeroplanes which the Board deemed most suitable for its route structure, the cost of Concorde was written off, and government interference was reduced to a minimum. It will take several years before the full benefits of the policy are realised but, in the meantime, the forward plans of British Airways in terms of future market trends, the assumption of freedom of entry in the early 1980s into what has been a heavily regulated industry, the composition of the fleet and productivity improvement plans—to mention but a few—have as much entrepreneurial content as would be shown by a comparable corporation in the private sector. Whether the management will be permitted to implement them remains to be seen.

VI. SUMMARY AND CONCLUSION

Let me summarise. Contrary to Rousseau, man is not born free; it is the genuflection he makes to his past that he is everywhere in chains. He has no choice of race, colour, creed or language; he has no choice, as Lady Bracknell would have put it, between being born into the purple of the trade union movement or forced to rise from the ranks of the aristocracy. The exceptional man shakes off some of the chains; but let us recognise that he is exceptional. Most willingly accept them and the routine life that results; most value highly job security in their chosen vocations; most harbour suspicion of change. Few display the entrepreneurial alertness stressed by Professor Kirzner; fewer still are capable of seizing the opportunity after it has been identified.

Although essentially an individual trait, entrepreneurship is not restricted to, and, in its more aggressive form, not all that common among, small businesses; it thrives in an environment where drive, energy and innovation are encouraged and rewarded; in an environment where managers are not only alert but clearly in charge of whatever destinies their corporations may have; in an environment where, as Max Weber once said, it is realised 'that man would not have attained the possible, unless time and again he had reached for the impossible'.[5]

---

[5] Speech made in 1915, quoted in Melvin J. Lasky, *Utopia and Revolution*, Macmillan, 1977.

Entrepreneurship will wilt where success is viewed with envy or contempt; where a spurious egalitarianism seeks to minimise rewards for initiative and effort; where the sheer weight of legislation and bureaucratic control becomes an albatross around the neck of the venturesome; where managements are demonstrably not in control of their enterprises, when their efforts for greater efficiency and profitability are frustrated by governments in pursuit of quite different objectives. It would be silly to state that entrepreneurship does not exist in nationalised industries; but it would be correct to state that its robustness usually varies inversely with the degree of government intervention; which raises again the question of why nationalise in the first place.

The Role and Purpose of Public Enterprise

P. D. HENDERSON
University College, London

The Author

P. D. HENDERSON: Professor of Political Economy, University College, London, since 1975. Educated at Ellesmere College, Shropshire, and Corpus Christi College, Oxford. Fellow and Tutor in Economics, Lincoln College, Oxford, 1948-65. Economic Adviser, HM Treasury, 1957-58; Chief Economist, Ministry of Aviation, 1965-67. Economist, World Bank, 1969-75. Author, *India: The Energy Sector* (1975). Edited *Economic Growth in Britain* (1965). Contributed to *The British Economy in the 1950s* (1962); *Public Enterprise* (1968); *Public Economics* (1969); *Unfashionable Economics* (1970); *The World Bank, Multilateral Aid and the 1970s* (1973); *The Economic Development of Yugoslavia* (1975).

Arthur Seldon: *Our discussion is opened by an English economist—well, he's half Scottish—who has been a British civil servant and an international civil servant too, and who has recently been writing on public investment programmes in Britain and also on the 'North-South dialogue'.*

I think I should begin with a confession, a confession of failure or at least of oversight. In University College London, where I now work, I give a course of lectures which is concerned particularly with government policies in Britain towards industries and enterprises, mainly those which are in the public sector but with some consideration also of the private sector. In these lectures I have never made any reference to the problem of entrepreneurship or the rôle of the entrepreneur; and in making no such reference I did not take a conscious decision to exclude the subject—it simply never crossed my mind to refer to it. Moreover, I suspect that if I had sent my lecture notes for comment to a representative group of fellow-economists who were likewise interested in this range of topics, while I would have received a wide variety of criticisms and suggestions for improvement, probably no one would have remarked: 'There's one rather important omission: you've said nothing about entrepreneurship'. Until recently, I had never heard of Professor Kirzner's *Competition and Entrepreneurship,* and I learned of its existence only by accident, not from a fellow-economist but from a reference in Robert Nozick's book, *Anarchy, State and Utopia.* Without consciously reflecting on the matter, I had fallen into thinking that the subject of entrepreneurship had disappeared from economics with Joseph Schumpeter's doctrine of 'the obsolescence of the entrepreneurial function', which was set out in his great book, *Capitalism, Socialism and Democracy,* in the early 1940s.

Thanks to the IEA's welcome initiative in choosing the topic of this conference, I was made to think again about the subject, and I read Sir Frank McFadzean's stimulating paper with great interest and enjoyment. With much of what Sir Frank says I am in agreement, but on the main thesis of the paper I was not at all convinced by what he says. As usual, it is much easier to be negative than positive, and it is the doubts and criticisms that I shall now concentrate on.

However, if I now summarise these doubts and criticisms, perhaps some of those present who, unlike me, have kept the subject of entrepreneurship in mind, and have thought about it constructively, will be able to play a more positive rôle—which incidentally would be most helpful for my course of lectures!

McFadzean's three classes of enterprise—and reasons for denying role of entrepreneur in nationalised industries

The McFadzean thesis, as I understand it, can be summed up as follows. We can think of the economy as consisting of three main classes of enterprise: small private businesses, large private corporations, and nationalised industries or public enterprises. As between the small businesses and the large private corporations, Sir Frank sees no essential difference with respect to the rôle and status of the entrepreneur. He believes that entrepreneurship, which he defines mainly in terms of the willingness and ability to undertake major commercial risks—which, however, have been carefully and responsibly assessed—is to be found equally in both types of business. He sees no reason to suppose that entrepreneurship is superfluous in large private corporations, or that it is in any way stifled within them. But between large private corporations and the nationalised industries he sees very big and alarming differences, for two main reasons.

The first reason is that (in his words), 'Nobody is clear as to what the purpose of nationalisation is'. The second is that, in Britain at any rate, governments have constantly intervened in the affairs of the nationalised industries in such a way as to undermine both managerial authority and financial disciplines. For both these reasons there is little scope for entrepreneurship in present-day enterprises. If however—so I interpret Sir Frank—governments were to behave more intelligently and more responsibly, and to permit the nationalised industries to act in the same way as large private corporations, to have the same commercial objectives and the same freedom of action, then entrepreneurship could and would flourish in these public enterprises, just as it does in private businesses both large and small.

I find myself uneasy about both aspects of the McFadzean argument, the private sector aspect and the public sector aspect. My terms of reference confine me to the public sector. As to the private sector, let me just say that Sir Frank does not seem to have answered Schumpeter's point, that in large bureaucratised private corporations entrepreneurial attitudes and functions have no place, and must gradually atrophy: 'Bureau and committee work tends to replace individual action'.[1] Sir Frank seems to assume that the existence of a profit-seeking motivation is in itself a sufficient guarantee that the entrepreneurial spirit will survive and flourish. I found myself wondering whether this was correct, and how one would decide the question.

As to public enterprises, which form the subject-matter of this session, my view is different from Sir Frank's. Let me begin by considering his first reason why entrepreneurship cannot be expected in these enterprises, which is that 'nobody is clear what the purpose of nationalisation is'. I believe that this is a mistaken view, and that the purposes of nationalisation as such, and the objectives of public enterprises, can both be defined in quite a straightforward way—though I have to admit that the ideas that I am about to summarise are by no means fully or widely accepted.

I would argue that the purpose of nationalisation can be analysed with reference to two related issues, namely:

(i) What ought to be the objectives of a nationalised industry or public enterprise?

(ii) What are the reasons which would justify the public ownership and operation of a business enterprise?

In answer to the first of these questions, Sir Frank would say, I think, that the objective should be the same as that of a large private corporation, namely, to maximise profits—if only governments would have the sense to permit this. If one takes this view, then there is not much of a case for public ownership and operation of any business enterprise, since the rôle and aims of such an enterprise ought to be exactly the same whether it is in private or public hands. So the answer to the second question is that there can rarely if ever be valid reasons.

I would answer both these questions in a different way, and I would like to set out my answers in summary form. The answer to the second question (the reasons for public ownership in the business

---

[1] Joseph A. Schumpeter, *Capitalism, Socialism and Democracy*, Allen and Unwin, London, 1943, p. 134.

sector) follows directly and immediately from the answer to the first (the objectives of public enterprises).

The purpose of nationalisation

First, I suggest that the right objective for a nationalised industry can be quite simply and straightforwardly defined. It is *to maximise profitability to society*: each public enterprise should be concerned with social profitability, as distinct from financial or enterprise profitability which forms the goal of a private corporation. From this the answer to the second question follows at once. The reason or justification for public ownership and operation of a business enterprise is that this is necessary, or at least highly advisable, in order to ensure that social profitability is maximised, in situations where under private ownership there would be a wide divergence between profitability to the enterprise and profitability to society. There are many reasons why the two may diverge, and nationalisation is by no means the only method of trying to bring them closer together. However, it *is* one possible method; it *may* in some circumstances be the most convenient and effective method; and the belief that it is so is to my mind the main justification for public ownership within the business sector of the economy, at any rate for those of us who do not object fundamentally to private ownership of the means of production.

This idea is of course very familiar to economists, and can, I think, be found quite clearly stated in Adam Smith. As an argument for public ownership in Britain, it has been cheerfully accepted by governments which were not in the least socialist in their ways of thinking: Dr Hannah reminded us this morning of the very interesting case of the Central Electricity Board, which was established by a Conservative government in 1926.

Now if we accept that social profitability should be the objective of nationalised industries, then it is misleading, or at any rate too simple, to suggest (as I think Sir Frank does) that the right course of action for governments is to allow and indeed encourage them to act precisely as though they were private corporations, and thus to have regard to financial profitability alone. But this raises a very real problem, which Sir Frank has quite rightly emphasised. If public enterprises are *not* left free to maximise their profits, what line of conduct should governments adopt in their dealings with these enterprises, and what should be the attitude and motivation of the managers who are placed in charge of them? Under the McFadzean system there are clear and (in principle) workable answers to these questions. Under the philosophy of nationalisation which I have just sketched out, what alternative answers can be suggested?

On this issue I detect two rather different strands of thinking among my fellow-economists in Britain, and I believe that each of these has something to contribute to a set of workable answers.

An artificial invisible hand

One line of thought is to view the problem of public enterprises as being to design a decentralised system of government control in which, largely through the impersonal agency of prices, public enterprises will be induced to act in the way that will maximise profitability to society. Public enterprise economics becomes an important particular application of the general principle of 'second-best optimisation', to use the jargon of our trade. Adam Smith, in a famous phrase, spoke of the invisible hand which could act so as to ensure that individual economic agents, in pursuing their own ends, serve at the same time the wider interests of society. The present-day theory of public enterprises represents an extension of this idea. It is concerned to develop rules which would provide, as it were, an artificial invisible hand, which would achieve the same beneficent result as the natural one in situations where the latter simply cannot function effectively. It thinks in terms of a 'corrected' market economy, in which one of the main economic functions of government is to bridge the gap between profitability to economic agents other than government, including the nationalised industries, and profitability to society. This should be the guiding principle for governments to follow in their dealings with public enterprises. This line of thinking has been developed in Britain in recent years by a number of authors, among whom I might mention Ray Rees, Ralph Turvey, and Michael Webb. It has had some influence both on the 1967 White Paper on the nationalised industries and on its 1978 successor.

Now *if*—and it may be a big 'if'—the government could devise a set of rules and conventions which would completely bridge the gap between social profitability and enterprise profitability, then

Sir Frank's doctrine would once again come into its own. Nationalised industries could be left to pursue commercial aims alone, and to maximise their own profits, since by doing so they would also, though not consciously or deliberately, maximise profitability to society.

The second strand of thought that I referred to is, however, sceptical about the extent to which this ideal can be achieved. It accepts that the objective should be to maximise social profitability, but does not believe that simply by rules and impersonal devices one can achieve a full reconciliation between the financial and social aspects. As a result, it takes the view that public enterprises should not think of themselves solely as businesses which are acting from commercial motives. On the contrary, there should be a conscious acceptance by the managers who run these enterprises that it is social profitability, and not just financial results, which ought to count. This point of view has been very readably set out by Alec Nove in his book, *Efficiency Criteria for Nationalised Industries*.[2]

Now both the groups of economists whose ideas I have tried to summarise agree with each other and with Sir Frank in one very important respect. They mostly believe, as he does and I do, that government intervention in the affairs of the British nationalised industries has in general been excessive and too detailed, and that a different framework of relationships is needed. At the same time, and whichever strand of economists' thinking one may prefer to emphasise, I submit that it is too simple to follow the straight McFadzean line, by saying that public enterprises should act in the same way as large private corporations, and that if they did a lot of problems—including, incidentally, the problem of entrepreneurship, with which this Seminar is concerned—would be solved. On the contrary, it may take a great deal of knowledge, insight and resourcefulness to establish conditions in which it would be right for nationalised industries to act as profit-maximising concerns, and there may well be cases in which these conditions cannot be realised in full. Where they remain unrealised, the aims *and motives* of public enterprises should in my view be different from those of large private concerns.

---

[2] Allen and Unwin, 1973.

Four concluding points

I would like to conclude by making four further brief points, as suggestions for consideration rather than as a considered programme.

First, I think that within the public sector there should be a deliberate attempt to make the structure and processes of management less centralised. Fewer things should be decided at Ministerial and Cabinet level, and more decisions left to the industries themselves. At the same time, we in Britain should be more flexible in our thinking about how public enterprises should be organised and run. It should not be so readily assumed that each industry should be a single monolithic unit, with all important issues decided at headquarters.

Second, decentralisation needs to be accompanied by measures to ensure more openness, and more accountability of individuals as well as organisations. I have sketched out a few ideas on this subject, which however are no more than a possible starting-point.[3] Much more thought is needed on it, both inside and outside the government departments and nationalised industries.

Third, and taking up Professor Kirzner's important point about freedom of entry, I would like to see the principle adopted that wherever possible the sphere of nationalised industries should be defined in such a way that other enterprises, foreign as well as British, could come into the industry and set up operations there.

Fourth, and more speculatively, perhaps we should bear in mind Schumpeter's idea that the main function of the entrepreneur is to overcome the environment's resistance to change. Schumpeter thought that this resistance was diminishing, and that this tendency partly accounted for the decline of the entrepreneurial function; but he added that

> 'the resistance which comes from interests threatened by an innovation in the productive process is not likely to die out as long as the capitalist order persists'.[4]

Wise words, indeed. But Schumpeter, working 40 years ago, did not foresee what I think I discern (though I am not sure that the sociologists would agree with me), namely, that people's capacity to

---

[3] P. D. Henderson, 'Two British Errors: Their Probable Size and Some Possible Lessons', *Oxford Economic Papers*, July 1977.

[4] *Capitalism, Socialism and Democracy*, pp. 134-5.

resist this kind of change, and the extent to which they can get sympathy and support from the rest of the community in their opposition to it, have greatly increased over this 40-year period. If this is correct, then in the modern world an especially important aspect of the entrepreneurial function, both in the private and the public sector, consists in finding ways of overcoming human resistance to change. I have no suggestions as to how this essential function might be better performed. But it is possible that organisations other than the private joint-stock company as we know it, whether these are publicly or co-operatively owned, may simply because of their status have some initial advantage in providing a climate and a setting in which the resistance to change is less determined.

Questions and Discussion

PROF. DAVID MYDDELTON (*Cranfield School of Management*): I want to make two comments. First, I have prepared consolidated accounts for the nationalised industries since nationalisation and I calculate that their total real losses amount to something like £35,000 million. What has depressed me is, first, that, as far as I know, no one in Britain is in a position to check whether my calculations are right or not, and, second, and far more important, no one in the country cares.

What the politicians have done by nationalisation is to destroy completely any criteria for discovering whether an enterprise is successful or not. The market economy has been called a trial-and-error system, but if there is no way of telling when you have made an error, you really are adrift. That is where I become very nervous about 'social profitability'. What does it mean? How do we define it? How can we calculate it? We are going to need social accountants to tell us whether we have made a social profit or a social loss.

Second, I would take issue with Professor Kirzner who seemed to me a little contemptuous about economic calculation. As a professional accountant, I give it rather a high priority. One of the interesting issues in this country, as in the United States and, indeed, all over the Western world, is the problem of inflation accounting. Without going into technical details on this issue, it seems to me that businessmen do have to make a more or less entrepreneurial choice between methods of accounting. They have to choose this method rather than that in order to judge whether they are really making a profit or a loss. Therefore economic calculation has perhaps more connection with the entrepreneurial function, in times of inflation at least, than Professor Kirzner suggests.

PROF. TOM WILSON (*University of Glasgow*): Professor Henderson said that it had not occurred to him very much to talk about entrepreneurship in his lectures on public policy. This is characteristic of nearly all of us in academic life. And it is not only a matter of academic interest.

We are training large numbers of people in theories of firms, the theory of industry, and so on. I suppose for the larger number of graduates in economics, a firm is two cost curves, a margin and an average, or maybe four if the student is a little more sophisticated. And there, by and large, it stops.

This procedure is quite serious since it gives a distorted impression of industrial life; and it is rooted in the emphasis on the static theory of the firm. Nicholas Kaldor argued many years ago, in a now forgotton article,[1] that perfect competition is inconsistent with static assumptions. He was absolutely right, but he did not go far enough. I want to enlarge upon that view. If you impose static conditions, you have eliminated not only perfect competition, but also the firm itself, because you do not need to have firms in a world of perfect knowledge or in a world where conditions never change—which amounts in the end to much the same thing. The decision-taking could then be done from the centre by some planning authority or, indeed, at any point from the centre down to the lowest level. The question of decentralisation is then redundant. Yet this emphasis on the static theory of the firm still flourishes and it is difficult to find text books which do not take this approach. I always try to reassure myself with the thought that perhaps we do much less harm to undergraduates than we might, because many of them do survive and become sensible people in spite of it, but nevertheless this is the kind of thing that goes on.

Related to this is the extraordinary view that in oligopolistic markets with a small number of firms there is no price competition. Five minutes serious thought will lead one to the conclusion that this is total nonsense, but you will find this teaching in book after book after book. So we do need a substantial change of emphasis there. When one begins by recognising that in a world where the future is uncertain, and where the entrepreneur must cope not only with risk but also with uncertainty—and so many things cannot be foreseen—in such a world one has to admit the necessity for a decentralised structure.

To comment on another of Professor Henderson's propositions: let us take a fully centralised collectivist economy, say, the Russian model,

---

[1] ['Market Imperfection and Excess Capacity', in *New Theories*, Vol. 2, No. 5, February 1935, pp. 33-50.—ED.]

and then see how even they have begun to decentralise. If you view the issue in this light rather than approaching it from the *laissez-faire* angle, it is extremely illuminating to see the need for decentralisation.

Then one comes to the point about market and social profitability. I was talking years ago to the manager of the investment bank in Yugoslavia (my interest was, of course, in regional issues such as Clydeside), and I asked him: 'Do you feel obliged to put a large proportion of your investments in Macedonia and Montenegro and the poorer areas, rather than farther north around Zagreb?'. He answered: 'Well, if the government wants me to do that, they must give me a subsidy and then I'll do it. Otherwise, I do what I'm told to do—I maximise my profits'. The point is that this policy is absolutely right, for various reasons. To take into account the various 'social' considerations that will not appear in the ordinary social accounts, like the old Pigou example of the emission of smoke, and so on, is absolutely valid. But then it is equally valid to insist that the government must be explicit about these 'social' considerations and subsidise or tax for those purposes accordingly. But let us not mix this up with the idea of running a business profitably. In Sir Arthur Knight's book,[2] he emphasised the need for manageable objectives and clearly stated aims for the firm, whether public or private.

A final point: I propose that no public money should be voted or passed on to industry merely on the recommendation of civil servants. This should be done only by the board of a nationalised industry or by a quango. I would then propose that all members of nationalised boards and of quangos ought to be required to invest x per cent of their personal capital in their industries. This modest proposal would, if adopted, have the most revolutionary consequences.

SIR FRANK MCFADZEAN: On this question of social profitability, may I say, as a businessman, that I find it difficult enough to run British Airways or Shell or Beechams or any other company with my eyes on the return on capital employed, and a few essential things like that, with my eyes on historic accounting, cost accounting, etc., without worrying about social profitability. I do not know what the social profitability of British Airways is, and I do not think anybody else knows either.

I was told, when I was chairman of British Airways, that the noise pollution round the airport meant that I should give compensation, or that compensation should be given, to the people who lived around the airport. But go and examine the prices of houses round the airport. Because there is more employment at the airport, house prices have shot through the roof. I do not know where the social profitability of that is. I

---

[2] [*Private Enterprise and Public Intervention: The Courtauld Experience.* Allen and Unwin, 1974.—ED.]

accept that there is a social cost to it, but that can be allowed for in the broader sweep of the subject. But I would not know how to run a business and then, at the end of the day, present my social profitability balance-sheet. You cannot run a business efficiently in that way.

PROF. HENDERSON: If Sir Frank accepts that there are some situations in some business enterprises where investments which would not be financially profitable to the enterprise would nevertheless be in the public interest, then, whether he likes the phrase or not, he is using the criterion which I suggested, of profitability to society. If as a manager in a public enterprise he goes on to say: 'Well, I'm not going to run my accounts in this way—if the government for its own reasons wants me to do something which won't pay, then they should see that my organisation's financial position does not suffer as a result, and make a payment to us accordingly' —if he wants to say this, I have no objection at all. But if he wants to argue that there are no occasions when the managers of public enterprises ought to think in terms of social profitability, and that return on capital employed is all that they should concern themselves with, then I think this is too simple a view. Let me ask him a question to illustrate the point. Supposing he had been in charge of London Transport in 1963, and suppose he had felt that the Victoria Line should be built even though from a financial point of view it could not be profitable to London Transport itself, how would he have tried to convince people that the scheme was worth doing and should be allowed to go ahead?

MCFADZEAN: I could not tell you anything about London Transport because I know nothing at all about its economics. I would need to make a study of it in order to reply. But there are 'social' costs in everything we do. There are 'social' costs if I leave my garden untidy; there are 'social' benefits if I have a beautiful garden; and so on. But in running a business you cannot take them into account. Now if the government says that I have got to have my aeroplanes smelling like Chanel No. 5, then the government would have to provide me with the Chanel No. 5 free of charge.

PROF. KIRZNER: I must correct a certain misimpression which, I gather from remarks both by Sir Frank and by David Myddelton, was that it was apparently understood that in my view the notion of calculation is somehow non-entrepreneurial. Let me explain the context again —and Professor Wilson's remarks can throw some light on this question.

The standard economic textbook approach, as Professor Wilson pointed out, is to imagine that the firm operates with a diagram in front of it, with a clearly marked and identified set of cost and revenue curves, and that somehow or other the problem is confined strictly to finding where the relevant curves intersect. In the real world, however, calculation never consists of that kind of task. Certainly, real-world calculation includes, inescapably and indivisibly, the task of *finding* these curves. And that is entrepreneurship in real-world calculation. The calculation which in standard economic textbooks is non-entrepreneurial somehow or other presumes that, by some miracle, each manager and each owner of each firm somehow or other *knows* exactly where these curves are without having to bother to make any decisions in the matter.

ARTHUR SELDON: I am not yet quite sure where the entrepreneur resides in a state enterprise, but at least I think I now know where he does not reside.

Now we shall learn where our saints and our sinners are. Some of you may know that my favourite academics are not sociologists. I doubt if cost-benefit studies would validate their massive and indiscriminate subsidisation at my expense and your expense as taxpayers. But there are exceptions: Julius Gould, who is in this gathering, is one; and Christie Davies, who is also here, is another; and Donald MacRae, who is about to speak, is a third. He will tell us of the sociological approach to the identification of sinners and saints, or villains and heroes, among our entrepreneurs.

5. From Villain to Hero?

DONALD G. MACRAE
London School of Economics and Political Science

The Author

DONALD G. MACRAE: Professor of Sociology, LSE, since 1961. Educated at Glasgow High School, Glasgow University, Balliol College, Oxford. Formerly Editor of the *British Journal of Sociology*. Author of *Ideology and Society* (1960); *Ages & Stages* (1973); *Max Weber* (1974).

I. INTRODUCTION

I begin with two observations. First, I agree very much with David Henderson that in-built, institutionalised and ideological Luddism is much more part of our society than it has ever been in the past. And I think I know why. I cannot quite see, however, why Professor Henderson thought that the mechanisms he suggested might do anything to alter this attitude. I wish I did.

Secondly, on social accounting: it is quite true, as Professor Kirzner said, quoting Ludwig von Mises, that all human activities are entrepreneurial. We all live by looking into the future, and by that definition all human activities must have an entrepreneurial aspect. It is a fact but, though it is an important fact, it is a fairly trivial truth, like the truth that we all breathe oxygen, which is only important if there is no oxygen supply. We do not need to state that fact in advance. It is also true that there are many institutions which have economic aspects—the family is an obvious one—which are capable of being subjected to some sort of calculus (call it social accounting, if you like)—they are genuinely economic but they can hardly be categorised in terms of business accounting, with or without the advantages and disadvantages and the quarrels over inflation accounting.

II. SOCIOLOGY AND THE ENTREPRENEUR

Now to my subject: the rôle of the entrepreneur, and his possible transition 'From Villain to Hero?'.

In English we have always been slightly troubled by the word 'entrepreneur', as has been made clear by Neil McKendrick. It is very clearly French, and has shown no sign of becoming anglicised. We can, of course, say 'undertaker' but that is altogether too funereal even for the dismal science of economics, far less the joyous discipline of sociology. The English translator of the French economist Jean-Baptiste Say, a sort of poet laureate of entrepreneurship, reverted to the older English usage of 'adventurer'.[1] Now that

---

[1] [On Say's emphasis on the entrepreneur, cf. Charles Gide and Charles Rist, *A History of Economic Doctrines*, Harrap, London, 1915, pp. 113-114.—ED.]

sounds all too dashing and somehow even dubious. So we are stuck with 'entrepreneur', or, as I shall sometimes say, in even older English usage, 'enterpriser'.

Sociologists' fear of entrepreneurial individualism

Now, my subject, sociology, which is not afraid of jargon, has been very afraid of 'entrepreneur', although I do not mean by that anything so vulgar as to suggest that a subject largely founded by, of all men, Auguste Comte[2] and Herbert Spencer,[3] is to be thought of as naturally socialist. The fear is of another kind. Sociology is the investigation, understanding and description of those devices by which social life of any kind is possible. It tends to be concerned in consequence with very ordinary things and people as a whole, and, as one of sociology's major modes of discourse is statistical, it tends not to be much concerned with individuals. But entrepreneurs are always, in their mythology, very individual, whether seen as heroes or as villains. Much of this mythology, demonology and hagiography is, of course, nonsense. Man, said Adam Smith, is an anxious animal. He is also usually a very prosaic animal. The great entrepreneurs, whether captains of industry or robber barons, or both at once, were—and no doubt still are—conspicuously exceptional, and even eccentric, individuals. The every-day entrepreneur, however, is not the robber baron. The every-day entrepreneur is not a captain of industry. He is fairly ordinary and not even much more anxious (though he may have cause) than the rest of us. He may perhaps have a certain indifference to risk, danger and anxiety and, indeed, also sometimes to the pains of others. In Samuel Smiles's great work, *Lives of the Engineers*, one of the things that immediately strike you is the degree to which all the great engineers (and most of those in Smiles's five volumes were also entrepreneurs) had a benign disregard for the sufferings of the immediate members of their family, their wives, their mothers or their children. There was also a certain hardiness, perhaps more than with most of us, but nothing else.

---

[2] [*Cours de philosophie positive*, 1830-42, and *Système de politique positive*, 1851-54.—ED.]

[3] [*The Study of Sociology* (1873), and *The Principle of Sociology*, Vol. I (1876). Modern treatments of Spencer's work include: S. Andreski (ed.), *Herbert Spencer: Structure, Function and Evolution*, Michael Joseph, London, 1971, and J. D. Y. Peel, *Herbert Spencer: The Evolution of a Sociologist*, Heinemann, London, 1971.—ED.]

Interest in social origins

It is here that we find the explanation of sociology's almost entire lack of interest in individual enterprisers. Only when it comes to the study of the social origins of business leaders have sociologists shown much interest. And that interest has been made legitimate to sociologists because one of our central concerns is that of social mobility and stratification, to which I shall return.

Sociologists have had a good deal to say about the environment inhabited by entrepreneurs. We may call that environment industrial society. We take it for granted, and quite rightly see it as something more fundamental than a distinction between capitalist and socialist economic systems, which are both based on industrialism. The working lives of employees on the shop floor or, indeed, in the managerial offices, I suspect, of Magnitogorsk or Turin, Coventry or Detroit, have a great deal in common. To the eyes of an Indian from the Upper Amazon or an imaginary Martian from science fiction, the lives of these people—middle management, supervisors, and shop floor workers—would appear pretty well identical. About this industrial order seen as a social system, sociologists have a great deal to say, as also of whence it came and whither it is going, not least in the theories of post-industrial society whose most distinguished exponent is Professor Daniel Bell.

Marx borrowed from Saint-Simon

The person who first understood anything much about the new industrial order was that very odd 18th-century fish, Saint-Simon. He was an aristocrat, a revolutionary, a financial speculator and a religious prophet. His disciples in France and Belgium were among the most daring, capitalistic entrepreneurs of the 19th century. Yet Saint-Simon is normally known as a socialist. He is claimed by the Marxists as an interesting but muddle-headed precursor of Marx's own scientific socialism. It is certainly true that Marx pillaged Saint-Simon with his customary bold freedom of intellectual enterprise.

Be that as it may, the core of Saint-Simon is that he observed something new that he called the emergence of a new kind of person, the *industriel* (and remember he died in 1825),[4] a term intended to

---

[4] [On this concept, originated jointly by Saint-Simon and his more liberal (and temporary) colleagues, Charles (not Auguste) Comte and Augustin Thierry, cf. Augustin Thierry, *Theory of Classical Liberal 'Industrielisme'*, Center for Libertarian Studies, New York, 1978, and the Preface by L. D. Liggio.—ED.]

embrace the whole body of workers, technicians, supervisors, managers and entrepreneurs who were at once creating and were created by the new industrial order and whose interests were, he believed, in fundamental harmony. Not least in this harmony were the bankers and financiers whose mobilisation of venture capital he regarded as central to the unfolding of the beneficial industrial society.

Samuel Smiles's heroes

So that, early in the 19th century—and here I trespass a little on some of the ground covered by Neil McKendrick—we can discern the four labels that were to be attached to the enterprisers. To some they were heroes. As Leslie Hannah said (p. 33), Samuel Smiles in *Self-Help* and *Thrift* and above all in the quite admirable *Lives*[5] of the engineers—I wish professional historians wrote so well and did such good research—saw them as heroes of will, virtue and ability, all of the most severe and puritanical varieties. But to others they were villains, like the financier who was central to Trollope's extraordinary novel about the corruption of financial speculation, *The Way We Live Now*, the least cosy of his novels, or Dickens's utilitarian Gradgrind, who, of course, were just as real as Smiles's great engineers.

To economists, however, and despite the fact that the IEA has brought before us such fascinating and amiable and interesting examples of the species today, entrepreneurs were and are somehow abstract. Economics is in its successes the triumph of abstraction. Individuals inevitably tend to disappear from economics. Entrepreneurs are necessary constituents of the market economy, of capital, production and distribution. They are constituents who could function well and who might function ill, but who remain essentially abstractions.

If the enterpriser were a monopolist, it was assumed on the whole that he practised ill. As I understand it, as a non-economist, it was not until the 1930s, in the two Cambridges, England and Massachusetts, studying imperfect or monopolistic or oligopolistic competition, that it was seen, as Professor Wilson said, that price competition did affect even the monopolists, and that they too

---

[5] [*Self-Help* first appeared in 1859, *Thrift* in 1875, and the lengthy series of *Lives* began with that of George Stephenson in 1857.—ED.]

might perhaps enjoy a drop of the mead of virtue. I doubt, however, if Mrs Joan Robinson, when she was writing *The Economics of Imperfect Competition*,[6] had this fall from grace in mind.

Entrepreneurship in agriculture

I should like to add here that there is one area in which entrepreneurship has always been regarded as thoroughly deplorable, and where entrepreneurs have always been given a bad name. That is the area we have not yet mentioned but which is one of our most successful and splendid industries: agriculture. Here, change in all received wisdom, judgement or myth is always held to be for the worse. Either the sturdy peasantry is being destroyed and the bold yeoman laid low; or the ancestral order of the village is being destroyed so that the squire and the pastor and the humble swain are put at sixes and sevens; or the independent farmer is being ruined by the bankers and loan-sharks and tax-loss people; or agri-business is threatening some sort of ecological doom. Try as we might, there is nothing that we sociologists can say other than that entrepreneurs are always villains with nothing to be said for them despite their apparently quite unpersuasive arguments that more people are being fed for less. The sacredness of rural life is impervious to wicked pleading of that kind.

Let us return to the wicked cities, and contemplate the four faces of entrepreneurship: heroic, villainous, home-made and the featureless enterprisers of the economists. But not everyone who believes himself to be an entrepreneur is one. We use the term in ordinary speech only for those who initiate business either *ab initio* or who expand it by new developments or new combinations, and who are, despite joint-stock enterprise, various forms of insurance, corporate conglomeration, and so on, at some real risk to both person and fortune.

III. THE VALUES OF INDUSTRIAL SOCIETY

What puzzles political, social and moral judgement is a combination of two elements. One is the comparative novelty—and this may sound very odd—of industrial society. In some sense we have known

---

[6] Macmillan, 1933.

about and lived in industrial society for a couple of centuries, and increasingly so. Yet its values are still altogether in debate, and the values we all hold, unexamined in the ordinary business of life, are derived from the insights of previous social arrangements, which pre-date those of industrial society.

We usually feel, wrongly, that there is something about enterprisers that belongs to an earlier, pre-industrial world, unless, of course, we are as robust as Sir Frank McFadzean. We feel somehow that enterprisers neither make nor serve. There was an old tradition in the pictorial drawing of Renaissance iconography that the figure of Time, the old man with a scythe, was always shown as a eunuch, because time merely re-arranged things and created nothing. People are not happy with an industrial society if it is not merely a society of novelty but a society almost unique in its human story, where real wealth per head has tended constantly to increase, and where there has been the possibility, therefore, of new autonomies, new freedoms, new creations and new wealth. Our values do not really belong to that world.

Pre-industrial sociologists

There is also a feeling that being 'on the make' is somehow a very ungentlemanly thing. But, of course, entrepreneurs are on the make, and that is clearly what they should be. But this perturbs sociologists. We feel that, if there is an important group of people in the society who are on the make, then the social order is at risk, that swindles are afoot, and that any general advantage is an unworthy by-product of the acts of the entrepreneur. That again is a pre-industrial set of judgements. Such judgements and values seem to indicate a fear that those wicked gentlemen—and I suppose they were wicked gentlemen—of the Middle Ages, about whom we were taught in elementary courses in economic history, are still with us. The forestallers, the regraters and the usurers were certainly very villainous, particularly in poor and marginal societies.

It is also true that entrepreneurship is today no guarantee of private virtue or public utility. Equally, of course, entrepreneurship is not an industrial order or the proof of vice or dis-utility. On the contrary: without the enterprisers, the industrial order would not exist, without the enterprisers, the industrial order would function less well, i.e. people would be poorer and poverty, which is, except for the saint, the enemy of autonomy and freedom, would be more universal.

Even Marx, after all, knew very well that enterprisers are a necessary price for the creation of industrial capitalism. Entrepreneurs, of course, are older than industrialism. The sociology of their creation, their risks, worries and rewards, has occupied some of the best minds in sociology in Britain and abroad. Within industrialism as a form of technology there must be new social and economic combinations and organisations, which involve entrepreneurship centrally and continually in the history of the non-communist world, and must go on involving it. But without it one can still have communist industrialism by centralised command. One can invent devices to mitigate this centralism, but command economies (and we have had 60 years of experience of them in this century) have not been pleasing in their results.

Robber barons at their worst—I speak here not as a sociologist but as an ordinary judge of human beings—were, it seems to me, really very preferable to commissars, but of course tastes differ.

Enterprisers—cause and consequence of industrialisation

Enterprisers were, then, both cause and consequence of industrialisation. But what about the 'technocrats', as they were broadly called by that very wry and shrewd observer of the industrial order, the man who first saw, as Sir Frank McFadzean pointed out so clearly, the penalty of being first in enterprise both for individuals and for nations, the Norwegian-American Thorstein Veblen, who died 50 years ago. What rôle should these technocrats, usually called engineers and technicians, play? The answer may perhaps be that they should substitute in some way for entrepreneurs, rationally making their decisions, rationally commanding and understanding the resources of the world of technology and of society, seeing as Oskar Lange, who has been quoted several times today (usually pejoratively), thought one might regard the entrepreneur—as a watchmaker or clockmaker who sees a clock in a glass case with every bit of the mechanism instantly visible and therefore the necessary adjustments to be made.

First of all, the technicians, technocrats, or technologists are already here in the industrial arts, and of course they are present centrally in most of our large, complex corporations. But, of course, the point about them is that they have quite specific technological, technical, technocratic tasks, and they are rewarded by being given rather smaller risks to bear than other people within the private, corporate, and possibly even within the public, sectors of the economy.

Also, in connection with my earlier point about the reason for the sociologists' neglect of entrepreneurs, I would suggest that it has to do with the individualism and eccentricity of the really interesting entrepreneurs, not the every-day, humdrum ones, or the ones who do something new but fall flat on their faces, or fail to change things very significantly. These people seem to have a certain kind of psychic adrenalin which the psychologists have not done much to explain, as it is perhaps inappropriate to the rôle of technician, technologist or technocrat. I shall deal with the technocrats towards the end of my talk when I discuss post-industrial society. Perhaps they are, after all, going to form a new socio-economic class. Certainly, entrepreneurs have never been, nor are they, a socio-economic class. One thing that sociology is quite good at is measuring social mobility precisely, that is, the movement of individuals. It is particularly easy to measure and to explain movement upwards, but rather more difficult to explain movement downwards. But it is possible. The movement of people upwards on whatever ladders of prestige, and therefore of influence, power and wealth there are in society, can be measured.

Social mobility, 1910-1960

But we do not find, at least in the period of which we have knowledge, which in Britain is roughly from about 1910-12 to the 1960s, that the entrepreneurs are at all homogeneous. They display a quite extraordinary diversity of origin, and they do not fit into the large categories which sociologists rather like. Britain and the United States are the two countries of any size which during that period had the highest rates of social mobility. Leslie Hannah's comment about the real history of our economic decline being a phenomenon of the Edwardian era to the 1920s with the pick-up coming in the 1930s, '40s and '50s, is rather more comprehensible.

We have seen diverse and high social mobility, especially among our entrepreneurs. Although climbing the ladder of success through small business enterprise has become rather more difficult, it is still possible, again as far as our figures show. They are still doing extremely well. And although diminishing, their rôle is still very important. Again, we would need to know more about the mortality of enterprisers before judging further on the probability of their continued success. My guess is that it is quite possible.

It also seems to me slightly surprising, given the very real incentives to small entrepreneurship in British society, that if you are interested in maximising your capital—real small capital, I am assuming—there are very real incentives in non-entrepreneurial areas like real property of a personal kind.

The entrepreneur in post-industrial society

It may be that we are moving towards the post-industrial society, described as one wherein the knowledge industry, the command of information, knowledge and technique, or, to use that old word of the 19th century invented, I think, by Matthew Arnold, a new technical 'clerisy', are coming into being, and perhaps even coming to form a new socio-economic class with internal solidarity, with habits of indogamy, with advantages of a kind that will ensure them differential access to education, privileged access to positions within this new technocratic clerisy. Even if all this is happening, and these things become central to the arrangements in what has been called post-industrial society, three very old-fashioned things contained in a child's primer of economics remain of importance: the need for (very often personal) risk-taking, the need for innovation (not the same thing as invention but connected), and the need for the mobilisation of resources and organisation.

In societies as diverse, as plural, as, for all that is wrong, ours is, even though the channels for entrepreneurial activity have certainly narrowed and changed direction somewhat, they are still there. I can see no particular reason as a sociologist for crying doom about all this, since I do not foresee the extinction of the entrepreneur any more than I see any reason to expect an extinction of the need for his functions.

It may be that we shall revert in the post-industrial society to seeing entrepreneurs as a kind of real hero once again, as conspicuous as were, in their own way, the entrepreneurs of Renaissance Europe. Perhaps Mr McKendrick's volumes, for which he is looking for one or two villains and failures, are the signs of a new pietistic literature in which, instead of the lives of the saints, the lives of the entrepreneurs will figure.

I believe with certainty that a post-industrial society based on the knowledge industries will otherwise follow Chinese society in many periods of the long history of Imperial China. It will become dominated by its mandarinate, and the fate of all mandarinates is rigidity and stagnation, tempered only by catastrophe. But, as ever, these entrepreneurs will, I think, go on originating diversely; nor can they as entrepreneurs form a class because their whole *raison d'être* is in their wry and eccentric individuality. They are people, after all, who clamber about the social framework and, of course, take the risk at times of tumbling down from it.

IV. SUMMARY: THE UNCHANGING ENTREPRENEUR— IN FACT AND FICTION

To sum up: entrepreneurs have not changed in public esteem from villains to heroes or from heroes to villains. By some they are still seen as devils, and this is not new. Entrepreneurs as usurers and extortioners, you may remember, were put in a special circle of Hell by Dante, along with the Sodomites and the blasphemers, and subjected to a reign of fire.

In fact and in fiction, some entrepreneurs have really gloried in trying to feel villainous. It is not just Andrew Undershaft in Shaw's *Major Barbara*, although his very interesting and important source was a man who did think about the economic aspect very seriously before thinking about entrepreneurs, but also real people like, for example, J. Gold or Jarvis Balfour, or all sorts of other characters in British and French economic and entrepreneurial history.

Entrepreneurs are no more and no less sinful than the rest of us. Sometimes their enterprises have been founded on public thuggery, sharp practice, ill faith or extortion. Sometimes, too, these things have changed as well as founded firms. Mankind on the make is often admirable but not often very seemly. But, as in theology, the devil himself is necessary to the design and purpose of creation, a servant, even despite himself, for good. This, too, can often be said about enterprisers. One main reason for this is to be found in a quotation from Adam Smith with which I shall conclude:

'The proportion between capital and revenue, therefore, seems everywhere to regulate the proportion between industry and idleness.
Wherever capital dominates, industry prevails. Wherever revenue,
idleness.'

The individuals who do something to prevent us facing Smith's
doom have been, warts and all, villainous faces and all, the
entrepreneurs.

Questions and Discussion

ANTHONY HOLLICK: Let us examine, say, Sir Freddie Laker. Over
and above any other person who is a statesman, a soldier, or a priest—
and certainly with a great deal more claim to public merit—Sir Freddie
Laker is both better-known and better-admired than the rest of this breed
put together.

FRANCIS MEDDINGS (*Retired banker; lecturer, Barclays Bank International, Institute of Bankers*): The notion of a hero or saint was really
irrelevant to Professor Kirzner's approach to the rôle of the entrepreneur,
which would seem to be a matter of identification and analysis. We are
not called upon to approve or to disapprove of the rôle of the entrepreneur,
but to discover this peculiar ingredient, entrepreneurship, in the complex
organisation of society. We are not asked to indulge either in hagiography
or in demonology. What we are asked to do is simply to see, among
other things, for instance, why Western societies on the whole display
rather more vitality than societies on the other side of the Iron Curtain,
and to discover what it is in Western societies that accounts for the
greater spontaneity and liveliness of our economic life.

ARTHUR SELDON: This is a matter of some importance. Why is it
that people like entrepreneurs, who seem to live by pursuing their self-
interest, but who, as is arguable, do social good, are regarded as villains?
Judged by their consequences, they are doing social good. Is there not a
confusion between entrepreneurial *motive*, which seems to decide public
attitudes and judgements, and entrepreneurial *consequence*? That was
the element I thought important for economists to discuss.

CHRISTOPHER TAME: Saint-Simon's concept of the *industriel* was
common among a large group of liberal economists and political thinkers
at that time who saw society divided into two classes, the workers and
the non-workers, except that, unlike Marx, they saw the entrepreneur

127

as the backbone of the working class, in practice the worker *par excellence,* and admired him thoroughly. For them the entrepreneur was a hero, the worker who created work for everyone else. This tradition existed for a time among a number of liberal thinkers, but has now been forgotten. I think it is one we ought to re-discover today. Fortunately, a large number of people are recapturing that vision and do not see soldiers and statesmen as heroes, but see businessmen as heroes, the true creators.

DR LESLIE HANNAH: The evidence I have from editing the *Dictionary of Business Biography* is that there is an inferiority complex among businessmen. When we approached businessmen for entries in the *Dictionary* and asked them about the contribution they have made, they invariably said they were members of a hospital management committee or contributed to the Conservative Party. If we tried to get them to say they have made money, they became extremely upset. This is a very deep-rooted social view, but I think it is perhaps wrong to see it as a general human phenomenon. It may well be simply a mutation which has afflicted this country.

PROFESSOR MACRAE: The point I am trying to make is that myths actually affect behaviour, including political behaviour and political decisions. If one believes in the general utility of entrepreneurs and entrepreneurship in society—and that does not mean one believes in all particular cases—then the myth of the villainous entrepreneur is an important and serious one. I know the Institute of Economic Affairs deals by definition with economic affairs and not with social or political affairs. But it is a sad truth, in all societies, for reasons that are not difficult to explicate, that the polity is stronger than the economy. In many societies, though not in all, in the long run social opinion is central to the working of a polity. These myths, therefore, seem to me of very interesting practical importance, as well as of proper sociological concern.

There is no reason, of course, why we should take the simple alternatives —hero or villain. Heroes and villains are not really, I suspect, the alternatives. The alternatives are about (to use a word Professor Kirzner used in a different context) primordial judgements of virtue and social utility. These things, again, are not explicable by economists: to a very small extent they are explicable by sociologists. I am concerned very much that inherited attitudes from pre-industrial, pre-lapserian society should not prevent us from judging and acting as realistically and effectively as we can in our present-day circumstances. And if that sounds like a Scots sermon, I am sorry for it. But there it is: if you ask a Scotsman, he turns political economy into morality.

6. Reforms Required for the Entrepreneur to Serve Public Policy

IVOR PEARCE

University of Southampton

The Author

IVOR F. PEARCE: Director of Research, Econometric Model Building Unit, University of Southampton, since 1973. Educated at Queen Elizabeth's Hospital, Bristol, and University of Bristol. Formerly Professor of Economics and Head of Department, University of Southampton, 1963-73. Author of *A Contribution to Demand Analysis* (1964); *International Trade* (1970); *A Model of Output, Employment, Wages and Prices in the UK* (1975). For the IEA he wrote 'Stimulants to Exertion . . . A Deficiency of Excitements', in *Catch '76 . . .?* (Occasional Paper 'Special' No. 47, 1976); 'Taxing the Dole', in *The State of Taxation* (Readings 16, 1977). He is a member of the IEA Advisory Council.

Arthur Seldon: *Our last paper is an effort at summing-up our day's work and asking: 'What does it all add up to?' We shall not agree on the content of all the earlier sessions, but at least we might now consider: 'What is there that government should do, or what should public policy be, to allow entrepreneurs to do what good they can do?' So we have Professor Ivor Pearce, who, unlike the economists and sociologists of earlier papers and the entrepreneurs, is an econometrician, to outline his view on the role of public policy.*

I. THE QUALITIES OF THE ENTREPRENEUR

No class of persons is so vicious as to be without virtue, nor is any so virtuous as to be without vice. Just now, therefore, when so many voices are to be heard proclaiming the supposed wickedness of the 20th-century entrepreneur, it is not inappropriate for a group of intellectual 'entrepreneurs' to organise a colloquium in defence of entrepreneurship. By the same token, however, it is not inappropriate for at least one speaker to remind the assembled company that the gains to society as a whole generated by entrepreneurial activity arise 'not from benevolence'. A captain of industry is not necessarily a philanthropist seeking to do good for others. More likely he is, in most respects, an ordinary human being, seeking to do good for himself. He is an unwitting catalyst, a bee whose strictly private activities are the first cause of almost everything else.

The world has a desperate need for entrepreneurs. It goes without saying also that the successful entrepreneur must have admirable qualities. He must be energetic, imaginative, courageous, knowledgeable and able to command respect. But he need not be unselfish, nor even honest. Leadership may call for skill, but it is not of the essence of entrepreneurship to know of and to promote everything that might be relevant to the wider needs of society.

An ordinarily clever bee might observe, and even claim credit for, the fact that his private honey-seeking serves also to pollinate. But only a very remarkable bee indeed could be expected to understand why the horticulturist sometimes shuts him out of the greenhouse, thereafter to proceed, with a paintbrush and much effort, to perform a duty which he, the bee, would happily have done for nothing.

The environment for entrepreneurship

The moral of all this is that it matters a great deal when and where and under what circumstances the entrepreneur can safely be encouraged to operate. The very qualities which create wealth in one environment serve only to destroy wealth in another Nor do entrepreneurs as a class much care about the environment, provided only it affords opportunities to pursue their self-interest.

For these reasons it is important to recognise that we are, today, seeking to rehabilitate entrepreneurship at a time when the environment in the United Kingdom is less suitable for the exercise of free enterprise than it has ever been in the whole of our history. The likelihood of abuse of the system is at its greatest. However much we may wish to see free enterprise restored, it is essential first to re-establish conditions under which it will work. That these conditions do not now exist it is easy to show, by example if not by comprehensive review.

II. INFLATION AND ENTREPRENEURSHIP

Entrepreneurship can never be suppressed, only misdirected, and there is no environment better designed to misdirect entrepreneurial effort than an inflationary one. When prices are stable it is impossible to earn an income without providing a service upon which the community places an equivalent value. Entrepreneurs *must* in these circumstances *produce* to live. In times of inflation, however, it is possible to make money without producing anything of value at all.

The profits of inflation: entrepreneurship without effort

Let there be two antique dealers, A and B, with stocks of 'art treasures'. If A sells to B, for £1,000, an object he bought from B for £100 and B similarly sells for £1,000 to A another object which he bought from A for £100, neither A nor B has any more money than before. Each has made a paper profit of £900, which can easily be turned into money. Any bank would lend cash on the strength of the increased value of both A and B's stock now authenticated by the transactions. Furthermore, interest on the loan can readily be paid out of the £900 profit turned into cash by the bank. The balance of profit is available for spending on consumer goods. As long as prices continue to rise, both A and B can live well without any real effort whatever; indeed without attracting a single customer to their auction rooms other than themselves.

This is not an impossible trick imagined by economists. It is happening now, ubiquitously, in Britain, not only in art but wherever commodities of any kind are held long enough for their price to rise, business or not. We cannot see it happen because most of those who benefit do not live exclusively on the proceeds of inflation. Their activities are masked by the presence of an occasional customer.

The art dealers in this fable were able to secure goods without providing a service, in precisely the same way as any common forger can enjoy the fruits of his forgeries. Those who produce commodities can always be robbed by those who gain a title to goods by fraudulent means. The only difference between forgery and commodity deals, in inflationary times, is that the banking system obligingly does the forging for us. More obligingly still, banks 'forge' only legal money, relieving the 'entrepreneur' who benefits from any fear of prosecution. The perpetrator of the 'fraud', which is not legally fraudulent, gains at the expense of the rest of the community.

Inflations favour trading, not production

Nor is this all. The *opportunities* for profit afforded by inflation are infinitely more damaging. The faster the rate of inflation the more profitable it becomes to use money capital to hold stocks rather than to buy productive labour. And it is in the nature of entrepreneurship to move quickly and efficiently from the less profitable into the more profitable. Production falls, buying and selling increases, prices rise faster still, and production falls again. It would be an exaggeration to claim that in the end everything is endlessly traded whilst nothing is ever produced, but this is only because the chaos created on the downward slide is always sufficient to reveal the facts of life, even to the most obtuse observer, long before the end is reached.

Those who argue that some degree of inflation is good for trade speak more truly than they know. It is good for trade but bad for production. As the madness develops, banking and trading activities reach unparalleled heights of frenzy—and everybody starves. *To provide an environment in which profit can be earned only by the production of valuable goods and services, the rate of inflation must return to zero and stay there.* This is not impossible, as the 19th century proved. But it is not possible unless our captains of industry understand that it is. Currently they do not.

III. PAYING WAGES OUT OF CAPITAL

Traditionally the entrepreneur has been the guardian of the nation's capital. He has not always been an entirely trustworthy guardian, particularly when the capital did not belong to him. Nevertheless, until the most recent times the system worked, more or less. Entrepreneurs did not preserve capital out of patriotism or for any other altruistic reason but in their own self-interest, knowing that without capital they could not survive. Nor is self-interest always enough. The classical example of the 17th-century 'South Sea Bubble' adventurer who issued a prospectus asking for capital for a purpose so secret that it could not be revealed even to subscribers sufficiently illustrates the need for legislation, which followed quickly upon the introduction of the joint stock company system. For many years it has been a criminal offence to pay *profits* out of capital. Paradoxically, it is not illegal, and it is common practice, to pay *wages* out of capital. For this reason the nation's real capital stock in manufacturing is probably diminishing—at an ever-increasing rate.

Using profits to buy off the unions

Why might it be to the advantage of the entrepreneur to diminish his capital stock to pay wages? The power of trade unions in some industries now borders on the absolute. Labour is able to say 'Pay or be closed down'. Entrepreneurs are aware that they have no money to pay by any rational calculation but they are equally aware that they have cash. In 1977 underlying profits of industrial and commercial companies were of the order of £12 billion; and gross trading profits were some £4 billion more than this. Only 10-12 per cent was paid out in dividends to shareholders, that is, about two to three pence in the pound of the Gross National Product.

At least £12 billion must have been retained by management to spend as they please.

In the ordinary way retained profits would be used for investment in the new capital equipment essential to replace worn or obsolete machinery. Without it the enterprise could not continue as a viable productive unit in the long run. What can the entrepreneur faced with irresistible wage demands now do? He may draw the attention of trade unions to the truths of costs and competitive product prices and refuse to pay higher wages, in which case he would be closed down at once. Otherwise he might postpone the evil day by paying the wage increase out of retained profit and allow the capital stock to decline. Any rational decision-taker must choose the second alternative. It allows him to carry on for a while, hoping that he might recover the position by charging higher prices in the following period, or that he might be bailed out by government hand-outs, or even, improbably, that wage 'negotiators' might come to their senses.

Retained profits pay wages; real net investment falls

Since 1973 something like 50 per cent of retained profits have been used to pay increased wages. This proportion is easily observed by noting each year the ratio of the rise in the value of work-in-progress to retained profits. In 1967 only one-seventh of retained profits financed wage increases. By 1973 the proportion had risen to one-half. In 1978-79 the situation will probably turn out to have been worse. We have high consumption at the expense of negative[1] real net investment.

Compare also real gross investment with wage-rate changes. Until 1970 real investment in fixed capital (gross of depreciation) in manufacturing industry grew slowly but surely. Wage increases (earnings) remained fairly steady at between 6 and 9 per cent per annum. Between 1970 and 1972 the earnings of labour rose sharply by about 25 per cent. Simultaneously investment fell catastrophically by 25 per cent. From 1972 to 1974 earnings rose slightly less fast (by 22 per cent). Investment recovered but only to a level 10 per cent below the peak of 1970. 1974-76 saw a huge rise in earnings of 50 per cent accompanied of course by a 20 per cent fall in real investment to the

---

[1] 'Negative' in the sense that fixed investment can be seen from the official figures to be less than is necessary to sustain production at current levels at a competitive cost.

lowest annual (1976) rate ever, expressed as a percentage of Gross National Product. Wage policies in 1976-78 checked the rise in earnings to 24 per cent. Real investment accordingly rose sharply. Throughout 1979 wage increases have again been high. The latest CBI investment survey is predictably pessimistic. We are approaching a new liquidity crisis.

If wage claims can be paid out of profits, restricting money supply must fail

The dangers of all this are two-fold. First and foremost, in the present situation, government attempts to apply monetary policy to reduce the rate of inflation are bound to fail. If the purpose of the present monetary policy is to force entrepreneurs to reject pay claims they cannot really afford by starving them of money, it will not work. It is of no use, in the short run, to reduce the rate of increase in the money supply if, all the time, industry is able to pay wage increases out of retained profits without new borrowing at all. The same quantity of money can be sufficient to finance higher wages and prices if the quantity of physical investment is reduced.

The second danger is obvious: if wages are paid out of capital the real capital stock must fall, production will fall with it, and the rate of inflation will *increase*.

Once again the self-interest of entrepreneurs will induce them to do what is bad for the country as a whole unless some change is made to the environment. What changes are necessary?

Reforms required to enable entrepreneurship to do its job

(i) If the 17th-century precedent were followed it might be made a criminal offence to pay wages out of capital. After all, to do this is to steal the property of the subscribers of capital by a trick no different in principle from that devised by the splendid confidence trickster whose prospectus was so secret that it contained nothing. If paying wages out of capital were made a criminal offence, it would be proper to imprison those who receive the stolen goods. The labour force would disappear—together with its generals.

(ii) A less drastic solution might be to restore the market for money capital which has been completely decimated by a succession of thoughtless policies. It would be necessary first to cease printing money. Industry must then be required to pay a rate of interest on the current market value of the most up-to-date equipment which will produce its planned output. (It now pays no interest on £12 billion of forcibly withheld profits.) In return industry should be allowed to borrow as much as it likes at the going interest rate. The rate of interest would have to be adjusted to equate the supply and demand for funds.

These simple rules would ensure that the community could not spend more than the value of its product whatever attempts to do so might have been made by various power groups. Wages could not be paid out of capital since entrepreneurs would know, or discover, that it is not possible to pay interest on money squandered in consumption. Trade unions could demand all they wished but they could have no more wages than the value of goods and services produced by their members.

It is not difficult to achieve all of these ends. More than one set of institutions could be devised which would have the desired effect. Nor would it be necessary to bring about any significant re-distribution of income in favour of one or other group. We might even come to understand at last the simple truth that poverty is alleviated not by investing less but by investing more, that is, not by consuming more as a nation but by consuming less.

IV. THE ENTREPRENEUR AND MONOPOLY POWER

No one has ever denied the obvious truth that markets do not operate to the public good in the presence of monopoly. If the system is to rely upon markets, monopoly must be eliminated. On the other hand, it is remarkable that conventional wisdom sees monopoly where it does not exist and fails to see it where it is present in the highest degree.

The scarcely challenged assumption that entrepreneurs are 'capitalists' and hence 'monopoly capitalists' is so far from the truth as to be ludicrous. The extent to which old myths persist which flatly contradict the evidence remains astonishing.

Capitalism and entrepreneurship are not monopolistic

Monopoly is the restriction of supply by a single seller in order to raise price. This definition does not fit either capital or entrepreneurship. If it is true that attempts are currently being made to raise the rate of return on capital by restricting its supply, they must be hugely unsuccessful. The real rate of return to capital at the present time, including retained profit, is clearly on the wrong side of zero. (Even Minimum Lending Rate at 17 per cent may not raise it much above zero.) Borrowers do not pay for capital; they are paid. Retained profits are less than necessary to keep real capital intact.

Entrepreneurs do not invest one block of funds in a project with a poor return merely to protect a very high rate of return enjoyed by another. Money is placed wherever the average rate of return is higher. However logical it might seem to an economist to equate marginal rates of return between the projects under their control, entrepreneurs do not do this. If they did they would no doubt proudly display the fact in their accounts, at least until the inevitable protests of financial institutions forced them to revise the policy.

Nor is there any organisation of entrepreneurs artificially restricting the supply of entrepreneurship. No examination is necessary to enter the profession. Nor does any management trade union set so high a price for its members' services that large numbers of them are left unemployed.

The real monopolists

The real monopolists today are the trade unions. Their power to restrict supply is absolute and for the most part legal. They do not fully succeed as monopolists because there are too many of them. In a world of monopolists, nobody is left to be exploited. Wherever there is power to exploit, but few potential victims, the result must be chaos. There is no solution to the problem of the irresistible force meeting the immovable object. By the exercise of monopoly power trade unions have managed only to consume a steadily increasing proportion of the capital stock of the nation, inconsistently proclaiming at the same time the 'right to work' of their members. There are two roads to destruction, and monopoly labour has managed to follow them both simultaneously.

Entrepreneurs are not without blame. They have failed utterly in the war of words. They must understand the absurdities they choose not to condemn, presumably in their own self-interest.

No 'right' to customers—or to work

Today's monopolists are not content with their monopoly. They demand also that their monopoly be described as virtuous. They claim for example to be defending the 'right to work' in circumstances where no such right could exist. Those who organise production buy labour in the market in precisely the same way that labour buys milk from the milkman. Monopoly suppliers of labour have no more 'right' to insist that producers should buy labour they have no use for, than the milkman has to insist that consumers should buy milk they do not want with money they have not got. The entrepreneur shopkeeper who demanded his 'right to customers' would be held up to ridicule by the very same persons who demand the 'right to work'. Yet the two things are the same. Both classes seek to survive by selling in the market the goods or services they have produced by their own efforts. Their rights, if any, embrace only the right to be allowed to trade in a market, free from physical coercion or threat of violence imposed by government or any other power (however secured), and free from conditions (monopoly agreements) designed to gain advantage by interrupting the free flow of trade.

Trade unions claim the right to engage in 'free collective bargaining'. One might as well say 'competitive monopoly bargaining' or 'black white bargaining' or any other pair of mutually contradictory adjectives.

Trade unions similarly claim that legislation is inappropriate in trade union affairs. All should be left to agreements freely concluded. Why does the government not instantly agree with them and abolish *all* existing legislation except that against violence and the restraint of trade? Monopoly agreements are always agreements in restraint of trade. Free trade may not guarantee the right to go on working when the product is of no value, but it does create the environment in which those who organise employment best flourish.

V. ENTREPRENEURSHIP AND POLITICS

The period 1945 to 1979 has been a very remarkable one in the history of the world. Every age has its political theory, but in none has the influence of the prevailing theory so dominated both minds and events as during the past 30 years.

The idea of the planned economy is as old as economic co-operation itself. The market economy, on the other hand, never began as an idea at all. It is simply what happens if no-one *has* an idea.

Failure of the planned economy

The planned economy, wherever and on whatever scale it is tried, always fails in the long run. It fails for one or more of three reasons.

First, the problem of communication is too complex. Money and prices have to be used, and come to be used, whatever the original intent. In the end the complexities become such that no-one, least of all the planners, can understand what the planning is achieving.

Second, people do not like to be told what to do. They prefer to think they are choosing for themselves, constrained only by economic factors which they see as part of the environment outside of anyone's control.

Third, and most important, a democratically planned economy, even if attained, is necessarily self-destructive in the long run. If there existed a government truly in control of the economic *status quo* and at the same time truly open to influence by the electorate, it would at once become more profitable to lobby the government than it would to produce goods and services. Production would slow and cease, giving way to a universal squabble for a larger share in a Gross National Product for that very reason rapidly shrinking.

The illusion of a planned economy

What has been remarkable about the period 1945-79 is not that we had a planned economy but that we thought we had. Two fundamental mistakes were made. First, it came to be believed that, to induce producers to produce, all that was required was consumer demand. It was taken for granted that production followed demand without capital, without saving or work-in-progress, without initiative and without entrepreneurship, in short, without effort of any kind beyond a little gentle labour. Second, it came to be believed that money did not matter. Money was seen as a tedious accounting device easily printed and useful only for generating demand.

The planned economy under democracy thus appeared, for the first time in history, to be feasible. The communication problem could easily be solved by channelling demand, frequently government demand, wherever there was a desire to see supply. Demand came to mean printed money. Saving became a bad thing because it seemed to mean less demand. In any event, if it should by chance be required, as much saving as we liked could be drawn out of an inexhaustible hat by producing more, that is, according to the prevailing theory, by still more consumption.

The entrepreneur disappeared entirely from the text-books of economics, being replaced by management whose only function was (apparently) to do the arithmetic necessary to calculate the technique of production which would maximise profit.

Politicians cannot 'plan'; entrepreneurs should give up politics

Economists became obsessed with a mathematical model. Entrepreneurs found themselves in the unenviable position of having to do the job that nobody any longer thought to exist. Inevitably *political* activity became profitable. Governments supposedly in control of the situation became lenders of last resort who could always find money as long as there existed banks to create it. Politics and banking have become our largest and most lucrative industries.

It is not yet clear how we shall recover from the present *impasse*. Nor is it yet clear precisely what damage the 1945-79 interlude has brought about. There are two things we do know. Before we can recover, governments must give up the pretence that they know how to 'plan' the economy. This of itself may achieve the second end. Entrepreneurs must themselves give up politics and return to their normal function. They must be recognised once again for what they are: the first among equals in the productive process.

PROPOSAL: A Challenge and a Weapon for British Entrepreneurs

I have been asked to say, in two minutes, what precisely I would wish to see government do, or undo, to avoid the almost certain failure in the short run of unsupported attempts to control the money supply. Very well. I would try to present British entrepreneurs first with a challenge and second with a weapon to meet that challenge. I have four points:

(i) To protect our capital stock from further deterioration we should announce at once that, at some specified future date (the delay being to avoid a liquidity crisis), it would be made much easier for equity shareholders (mostly insurance companies, pension funds and financial institutions) to withdraw their capital *at its true value*, just as all employees are free to withdraw their labour. Each quarter, shareholders should be advised of the net worth of their company at current prices and their share in the equity. If in the light of this information any shareholder wished to withdraw his capital the company should be required to pay his share of net worth, in cash, on demand, less a fixed percentage (say, 10 per cent) to discourage trivial withdrawals. This obligation would be subject, of course, to the usual rules of bankruptcy and ranking of creditors.

Rule (i) would ensure that dividends plus retained profits together yield on the average at least the going rate of interest. Wages could not then be paid out of capital. The 'owners' of the means of production would once more be identifiable and possessed of sufficient power to protect, in some degree, their, and the nation's, capital. Companies in difficulties would be forced more quickly into liquidation or reconstruction, that is, to respond more rapidly to change. Shareholders and the work-force would be pressured into agreements for self-preservation. Trade unions in failing industries might come to understand, perhaps, that, where there is insufficient revenue from production, more long-run benefit might be derived from wage cuts rather than wage increases.

(ii) The concept of 'agreement under duress' should be introduced into industrial relations. If any party to an agreement feels that he was forced to accept its terms 'under duress' he may so declare and, by that declaration, render the agreement null and void. All parties *must* then go at once to arbitration. The only matter the arbitration board should be empowered to consider is 'ability to honour the agreement without endangering the continuance of the business'. In determining their ruling on this, the arbitration board's calculations must be made at those prices and costs obtaining at the date of the agreement. The 'justice' or 'injustice' of the agreement should not be considered by the board. It should be empowered only to confirm or abrogate the agreement on the single criterion of 'ability to pay'. If the agreement were nation-wide, any small company might be free to declare 'duress' and prove its inability to pay. Similarly, any local trade union official might prove 'duress' and so obtain for his members wage increases higher than those agreed nationally.

(iii) It goes without saying that rules (i) and (ii) above must be supported by a balanced budget, by strict control of the money supply and, as a corollary, the abandonment of all attempts to control the interest rate. The first symptom of a proper control of the money supply would be a rise in interest rates to something a little above the expected rate of inflation. The house mortgage problem can easily be handled by requiring building societies to make real rather than nominal contracts. Taxes should be levied only on *real* capital gains and the *real* rate of interest.

(iv) There should be wide public discussion of the effects of policies (i), (ii) and (iii) on the distribution of income. The electorate must be told over and over again that almost all equity in the UK is held by insurance companies, pension funds and other financial institutions. Dividends on ordinary shares paid in 1978 to persons, as opposed to financial institutions,[1] could hardly have been more than *one-tenth* of the amount spent by consumers in 1978 *on alcoholic drinks alone*.[2] The most significant effect on income distribution of the changes above would almost certainly be to make it possible for pensions and insurance benefits to be inflation hedged. The inflation itself could not for long continue.

Questions and Discussion

ARTHUR SELDON: I think our comments ought to concentrate on what public policy ought to be to enable the entrepreneurs, fallible though they are, to do their best work. In so commenting we ought to bear in mind an aspect of importance in recent months, namely, what do you do if government not only does not want to do these things, or is incapable of doing them, but is obstructed from doing them, not least by its own bureaucracy? What does one do if a government that wants to vary the framework of laws, etc., to enable the entrepreneur, or induce him, to respond to changing demand, is itself obstructed?

PROF. CHARLES ROWLEY (*University of Newcastle upon Tyne*): Professor Pearce picked up a very important point when he mentioned

---

[1] Central Statistical Office, *National Income and Expenditure: 1979 Edition* (Blue Book), HMSO, 1979, Table 5.4.

[2] *Ibid.*, Table 4.9.

that the returns to entrepreneurship at the present time are much greater in the political than in the economic arena. We know this to be true in Britain, and in my view it is true also in the USA. Once the system has been so developed that people see that pork-barrel politics pays, as President Carter is himself finding out now in the pre-run to the election period—the man who comes in to stop the pork-barrel, so to speak, is now becoming a part of that establishment and is responding to those very pressures. Once this happens it becomes extremely difficult to remedy, because the best entrepreneurs are now directed into pressure-group lobbying, i.e. into entrepreneurial behaviour in the political system, and are drawn away from activities of low return.

If we accept that premise, and if the politicians accept it and want to do something about it, they have to move to constitutional solutions to constrain themselves and their powers, so that the entrepreneurs no longer see gain from the political system. The politicians and the electorate in California have constrained themselves from taxing through realty taxes and have put pressure upon the Government of the State to lower the rate of public expenditure. This is possible; and there is a movement in the United States at the moment which derives much of its impetus from Proposition 13, and which other States are beginning to recognise. It is one weakness of Mrs Thatcher's Government at present that she is not in this sense a constitutionalist, but an adherent of parliamentary sovereignty. She is thus leaving herself exposed to pressure-groups and obstructors because she has no answer when they say: 'You can do this'. If her answer were: 'I cannot do it, since my government is limited by the constitution', she could re-direct entrepreneurial activity back to the market. That would be at least a part of the solution of preventing government from being pressurised by political entrepreneurs.

PROF. DAVID MYDDELTON: My solution is much the same as Professor Pearce's, namely, *laissez-faire*. As an accountant who now teaches economics, I know how difficult it is to move from the one subject area to the other. I was a little nervous at some of Professor Pearce's accounting ventures.

On constitutional methods, I hope Lord Hailsham, the present Lord Chancellor, will have the courage of his convictions and stick with what he used to say continually in opposition and introduce a Bill of Rights. There is no one in the country in a better position to do so, and if he really meant what he said I hope he will get on with it.

Two last observations. First, meaning well is not the same as doing good, which may have an awful lot to do with the public image of the entrepreneur, who does not set out to mean well in any public way, and yet may be doing us all good. Secondly, on government policy, the government should not try to do good. I would be more than satisfied, and incredibly relieved, if it would simply not do harm. That is an ambitious task for government.

DR LESLIE HANNAH: Allow me to enter a caveat on the constitution approach. In a number of areas which affect entrepreneurship, it is difficult to envisage a constitutional change having quite the dramatic effect which some speakers have suggested. For example, one of the problems which afflict small entrepreneurs in getting capital from the capital market (with some exceptions) is that our tax system gives strong incentives for people to save their money in pension funds, insurance companies and housing, and not through productive industry. It is not at all obvious how you can draft a constitution to prevent that diversion. Nor is it obvious that it is fair to the insurance companies to change that now. They have, after all, taken a fantastic entrepreneurial opportunity, which was to use the belief that insurance is a good thing to get enormous sums of money from the public, and they have been rewarded for it. In short, they have shown entrepreneurship, but have been guided in the wrong direction. It has done social damage, perhaps; but there remains a problem of vested interest. It really is wrong to hit entrepreneurs on the head and suddenly to change direction when they have been responding to perfectly lawful incentives. And there is no sense in which we can claim that taxing insurance companies is constitutionally right and not taxing them is wrong.

There is no sense in which you can define a constitution properly to avoid distortions of this kind, because there is no neutral state: a tax on, or a tax off, is something that requires discussion; it is impossible to define it constitutionally. So we really are stuck with these problems of devising the right kind of institutional framework, whether we like it or not. The constitution is not an easy solution—it is simply a re-statement of the fundamental problem.

DR RALPH HORWITZ: May I try very briefly to defend my position against Professors Pearce and Kirzner. One of this morning's guests was, at the bottom of the Depression in 1930, the nephew of an uncle who, standing very alertly outside the trying-on room, heard his salesgirl having difficulty in concluding a sale because the customer had insufficient cash. The uncle intervened to ask: 'How much have you in your purse?' The customer said: '10 shillings—and I can pay off the balance'. My friend of this morning went on to develop the weekly payment system for clothing so that turnover is currently tens of millions. When he asked my advice on how to float his company, it was in the days when profits did return to the capital market as dividends, and he was able to become a very successful entrepreneur indeed.

My point is that to open up the capital market to managers who wish to become entrepreneurs is a key reform, but the dynamics of the 'model' are more meaningful in terms of entrepreneurial management than in terms of entrepreneurship.

R. KELF-COHEN (*Retired civil servant*): The prevailing view at this gathering is that the free flowering of entrepreneurial enterprise is destroyed by government bureaucrats; it has even been suggested that such activity is their main purpose in life.

For 30 years I served in Departments of State which dealt with economic affairs and in the course of those years I had contacts with almost every major industry. My experience has been that the industrialist does not complain of state interference. On the contrary, he seeks its help. It may be a matter of quotas, tariffs, access to foreign markets, grants-in-aid, and so on. I retired some time ago but, to the best of my knowledge, this state of affairs has not changed; it has only increased. Need we mention Ferranti, Alfred Herbert, Rolls-Royce and British Leyland? Is not the present Government trying to change this state of affairs?

PROFESSOR KIRZNER: I must confess that during all the very stimulating discussions I have heard today it seems that a rather significant aspect of entrepreneurship has somehow been overlooked. Much of the discussion has concentrated on the successful businessman, the brilliant innovator, the possibly heroic character of the entrepreneur, the circumstance of Professor Pearce's observation that the entrepreneur may have more money than the rest of us. This presents the entrepreneur as a flesh-and-blood individual, the big businessman. Our Chairman referred to entrepreneurs at one stage as 'capitalists'.

All of this leads us perhaps to overlook the very important distinction between the flesh-and-blood businessman, *the* entrepreneur, on the one hand, and the entrepreneurial rôle, on the other. One speaker was somewhat sceptical of the term 'entrepreneurship', and his association of it with other kinds of 'ships' led me to suspect that he thought entrepreneurship was full of hot air. But the very term 'entrepreneurship' has an important contribution to make because it focusses not on the flesh-and-blood individual who is a businessman but on the entrepreneurial *role*, which is indeed present in everyone.

We are all entrepreneurs. The trade union leader is an entrepreneur, too, since, as was pointed out, political entrepreneurship is very much part of entrepreneurship. The leader in a nationalised industry is also called upon to exercise entrepreneurship. The distinction between the businessman entrepreneur and the others is in a way somewhat unfortunate.

Much has been made today of change, of the entrepreneur as innovator in the Schumpeterian sense—and, as you may recall, to Schumpeter the entrepreneur was indeed an heroic figure. But one of the shortcomings of Schumpeter is that his entrepreneur was one who dealt only with big, heroic changes. Yet entrepreneurship is required for little just as much as for big changes. Economic progress need not necessarily involve big, dramatic, heroic innovation and change. It may consist of pedestrian little steps and changes, which may not seem heroic to anyone but which may call for the very same qualities of entrepreneurship on a small scale as the big business successes. I must agree with Mr Meddings's remark earlier this afternoon that whether the entrepreneur is hero or villain is beside the point, and this is especially so when one deals with the entrepreneur not in the sense of a flesh-and-blood individual but in the sense of the entrepreneurial rôle. This term is an analytical concept; it comes integrated and packaged with every other kind of human characteristic, with every other kind of analytical rôle—the observable flesh-and-blood individual is only partly an entrepreneur, as are we all.

Where does it all lead? I agree with Professor Pearce that what is required is, finally, the entrepreneurial environment, which encourages entrepreneurship, in terms of little changes as well as of big changes. That kind of environment is exactly *laissez-faire*, 'get off our backs'.

ARTHUR SELDON: It now remains for me to ask you to thank all 10 of our speakers, and for me to thank you for your questions, your comments—or your silence.

RUSSELL LEWIS: May I venture on behalf of the audience to thank you, Mr Chairman, for the splendid way in which you have guided our discussions, and the IEA staff for their efficient arrangements in looking after both our enlightenment and our comfort.

List of Participants at IEA Colloquium on 'The Role of the Entrepreneur' *(22nd October 1979)*

ALEXANDER, JAMES, *London School of Economics (Student)*
ANDERSON, DR D., *University of Nottingham*
ASHTON, MICHAEL J., *Ashton & Moore Limited*

BALDWIN, B. A., *Price Waterhouse & Company*
BALLARD, P. C., *Roche Products Limited*
BAYER, S., *Argentina*
BRYANT, JOHN, *Executive Editor, Daily Mail*
BURN, DUNCAN, *IEA Author*
BURRELL, M. J., *Merrick Burrell & Partners Limited*
BURTON, JOHN, *University of Birmingham/IEA Author*
BUTLER, IAN G., *Lead Industries Group Limited*

CAINE, MICHAEL, *Booker McConnell Limited*
CAINE, SIR SYDNEY, *IEA Author*
CARTER, ROLAND, *Civil Servant*
COATES, I. L., *The Guthrie Corporation Limited*
COATES, J. B. M., *Coates Brothers*
CORLEY, T. A. B., *University of Reading*
CRISP, JASON, *Financial Times*

DAVIES, ALUN, *Rio Tinto Zinc*
DAVIES, CHRISTIE, *University of Reading*
DRIVER, J. C., *University of Birmingham*

ELKAN, PROFESSOR WALTER, *Brunel University/IEA Author*
EVELY, RICHARD, *Regional Development Analysts Ltd.*

FERNIE, W. M., *Whitbreads*
FERNS, PROFESSOR H. S., *University of Birmingham/IEA Author*
FISHBONE, IVOR, *Self-employed*
FRY, RICHARD, *Retired City Editor*

GILBERT, IAN, *Baker Perkins Holdings Limited*
GOLT, SIDNEY, *Adviser on Commercial Policy, International Chamber of Commerce*
GOULD, PROFESSOR S. J., *University of Nottingham*
GRIMWADE, ALFRED, *Grove Charity Management*
GURZYSKI, PROFESSOR Z., *London School of Economics*

HAINSWORTH, S. B., *J. H. Fenner & Company*
HAMPSON, C., *ICI Limited*
HANNAH, DR LESLIE, *London School of Economics*
HARDING, R. W., *Marks & Spencer*
HART, DR, *University of Southampton*
HARRIS, ROBIN, *Conservative Research Department*
HENDERSON, PROFESSOR P. D., *University College, London*
HILDRETH, JAN

HILTON, IAN, *London School of Economics (Student)*
HINTON, D. I. S., *BICC Industrial Products Limited*
HOLLICK, TONY, *Research Officer, Alliance of Small Firms and Self-employed People*
HOPPE, MALCOLM, *Aims—the Free Enterprise Organisation*
HORWITZ, DR RALPH, *London Regional Management Centre*
HUXLEY, GERVAS, *Student*

JULIER, NORMAN N., *Geltsdale Textile Industries Limited*

KANBUR, S. M., *University of Cambridge*
KAVANAGH, N. J., *University of Birmingham*
KELF-COHEN, R., *Retired Civil Servant*
KIRZNER, PROFESSOR ISRAEL M., *New York University*
KNIGHT, SIR ARTHUR, *Courtaulds Limited*

LEWIS, RUSSELL, *Daily Mail/IEA Author*

MCFADZEAN, SIR FRANK, *Shell Transport & Trading*
MCKENDRICK, NEIL, *Gonville and Caius College, Cambridge*
MCKENZIE, COLIN, *Business man*
MACRAE, PROFESSOR D. G., *London School of Economics*
MARGOLIS, CECIL, *Cecil Margolis Limited*
MARSHALL, M. D., *Cadbury Schweppes*
MARSHALL, MISS PAULINE, *NE London Polytechnic (Student)*
MEDDINGS, FRANCIS, *Retired Banker*
MICHAELS, PAUL, *Business man*
MØLLER, E. N., *Shell International*
MYDDELTON, DAVID, *Cranfield School of Management/IEA Author*

NICOLAIDES, MRS ERI, *Trade Policy Research Centre*

ORCHARD, L. W., *Berec Group*

PEARCE, EDWARD, *Daily Telegraph*
PEARCE, PROFESSOR IVOR F., *University of Southampton/IEA Author*
POLLECOFF, BERNARD, *Sallek Chemical, S.A.*
PRESS, SIDNEY, *Edgars Ltd*
PRICE, E. H. M., *Department of Industry*

RANTALA, MISS LAURI, *London School of Economics (Student)*
REED, C. T., *Cecil Margolis Limited*
RICKETTS, MARTIN, *University College at Buckingham/IEA Author*
ROBBINS, LORD
RODERICK, PROFESSOR GORDON, *University of Sheffield*
ROWLEY, PROFESSOR CHARLES, *University of Newcastle/IEA Author*
RUBNER, ALEX, *Economist/Author*

SACH, D. S., *I.C.F.C. Limited*
SEWILL, BRENDON, *Committee of London Clearing Bankers/IEA Author*
SHAKERLEY, C. T. E., *Provincial Insurance Company Limited*

SHARP, ERIC, *Monsanto Limited*
SIMON, PETER, *Legal & General Assurance Society Limited*
SLATER, G. S., *Berger, Jenson & Nicholson Limited*
SLATER, J. R., *University of Birmingham*
SLOANE, PROFESSOR P. J., *Paisley College/IEA Author*
SMITH, GRAHAM, *Research Officer, Freedom Association*
SMITH, SIR LESLIE, *BOC International Limited*
STEPHENS, PROFESSOR MICHAEL, *University of Nottingham*
SUTHERLAND, BRUCE, *Harris & Sheldon*

TAME, CHRIS, *Alternative Bookshop*

VINSON, NIGEL, *Plastic Coatings*

WALLER, WALTER, *Lucas Industries*
WALLIS, M. T. J., *Midland Bank*
WASSELL, MARTIN, *International Chamber of Commerce, Paris*
WATES, CHRISTOPHER, *Wates Bros.*
WEBLEY, SIMON, *British North American Research Centre*
WICKENDEN, KEITH, *European Ferries*
WILKINS, G. J., *Beecham Group Limited*
WILLEY, J. A., *Berger, Jenson & Nicholson, Limited*
WILSON, PROFESSOR THOMAS, *University of Glasgow/IEA Author*
WORSTHORNE, PEREGRINE, *Sunday Telegraph*

YAMAMURA, NOBUYUKI, *Long Term Credit Bank of Japan*
YOUNGMAN, D. J., *Coates Brothers*

IEA READINGS in Print

1. Education—A Framework for Choice
Papers on historical, economic and administrative aspects of choice in education and its finance
A. C. F. Beales, Mark Blaug, E. G. West, Sir Douglas Veale, *with an Appraisal by* Dr Rhodes Boyson
1967   Second Edition 1970 (xvi+100pp., 90p)

2. Growth through Industry
A re-consideration of principles and practice before and after the National Plan
John Jewkes, Jack Wiseman, Ralph Harris, John Brunner, Richard Lynn, and seven company chairmen
1967   (xiii+157pp., £1·00)

4. Taxation—A Radical Approach
A re-assessment of the high level of British taxation and the scope for its reduction
Vito Tanzi, J. B. Bracewell-Milnes, D. R. Myddelton
1970   (xii+130pp., 90p)

5. Economic Issues in Immigration
An exploration of the liberal approach to public policy on immigration
Charles Wilson, W. H. Hutt, Sudha Shenoy, David Collard, E. J. Mishan, Graham Hallett, *with an Introduction by* Sir Arnold Plant
1970   (xviii+155pp., £1·25)

6. Inflation and the Unions
Three studies on the effects of labour monopoly power in Britain and the USA
Gottfried Haberler, Michael Parkin, Henry Smith
1972   (xii+88pp.; available on microfiche only: £3·50)

8. Inflation: Economy and Society
Twelve papers by economists, businessmen and politicians on causes, consequences, cures
Lord Robbins, Brian Griffiths, J. A. P. Treasure, D. R. Myddelton, Raymond Fletcher, Paul Bareau, Henry Smith, Andrew Alexander, Richard Lynn, Lewis Whyte, Nicholas Ridley, Graham Hutton
1972   (ix+136pp.; available on microfiche only: £3·50)